Climbing the Ladder

Climbing the Ladder (1986) looks at the fundamentals for women breaking the glass ceiling, examining the barriers to progress and the ways to success. It focuses on the barriers placed by the company itself (its history, structure and attitudes); by men both in the office and in private life; and by the women themselves – self-confidence, for example. It looks at career planning and home life management, and draws out useful insights into the possibilities of progress.

Climbing the Ladder

How to be a Woman Manager

Janet W. Macdonald

Routledge
Taylor & Francis Group

First published in 1986
by Methuen London Ltd

This edition first published in 2025 by Routledge
4 Park Square, Milton Park, Abingdon, Oxon, OX14 4RN

and by Routledge
605 Third Avenue, New York, NY 10017

Routledge is an imprint of the Taylor & Francis Group, an informa business

Publisher's Note
The publisher has gone to great lengths to ensure the quality of this reprint but points
out that some imperfections in the original copies may be apparent.

Disclaimer
The publisher has made every effort to trace copyright holders and welcomes
correspondence from those they have been unable to contact.

A Library of Congress record exists under ISBN 0-413-60070-X

ISBN: 978-1-032-93843-1 hbk)
ISBN: 978-1-003-56790-5 (ebk)
ISBN: 978-1-032-93848-6 (pbk)

Book DOI 10.4324/9781003567905

JANET W. MACDONALD

Climbing the ladder
How to be a woman manager

METHUEN

First published in Great Britain 1986
by Methuen London Ltd
11 New Fetter Lane, London EC4P 4EE
Copyright © 1986 Janet W. Macdonald

Printed in Great Britain by
Richard Clay (The Chaucer Press) Ltd,
Bungay, Suffolk

British Library Cataloguing in Publication Data

Macdonald, Janet W.
  Climbing the ladder: how to be a woman manager.
  1. Women executives   2. Success
  I. Title
  658.4'09   HD6054.3

  ISBN 0–413–60030–0
  ISBN 0–413–60070–X Pbk

For Ken

who is all the things a working woman needs in a husband

Contents

Preface

'Women in management' is a subject which is currently fashionable and always good for a few column inches in newspapers, not to mention doctoral theses among sociologists. There have been many recent academic studies on the problems of women managers, the stresses and pressures to which they are subject, the generally low percentage of women in management and suggestions that the onus for correcting this situation should lie with employers.

No doubt this is true, but it presupposes that employers care. If they genuinely want to help their female employees, all is fine. But what of those employers who feel that their management needs can be satisfied by recruiting from the large, experienced male work-force available? Many employers feel little motivation to devote money and energy into providing training programmes aimed specifically at women.

I believe that it is up to us women to shift for ourselves and make sure we are fitted for the jobs we seek, rather than expect someone else to do it.

When I found myself in the position of wanting to start my career climb a few years ago, I looked for a book to give me the advice to help me – and failed to find one that was relevant. There were many academic studies of women who had made it to the top; and there were several American imports on office politics, but there was nothing which actually set out the basic principles needed to build a career in management.

The more books I read and the more courses I attended in the search for the answers to my ladder-climbing problems, the more I became convinced that these answers should be available in one book written by a woman who knew what she was writing about from first-hand experience. And since no one else seemed to be producing one, I thought I had better do it myself.

I am not a sociologist or a professional journalist or a career guidance consultant. I am an accountant employed by a big international organisation – a working girl, just like you. I am halfway up my chosen ladder and I intend to get to the top. I see no reason why you should not do the same – and I hope this book makes your climb easier than mine.

October 1985

Author's note
In the interests of clarity, I have used the word 'company' to include all the places where a manager might work, such as the Civil Service and professional firms, as well as commercial organisations.

Introduction

We live in a society where more people work with their brains than with their hands. Sheer brute strength is no longer a valid test of superiority – not that it ever has been in an office environment – and yet half the available work-force is grossly under-utilised on the basis that it is incapable of doing as good a job as the other half.

I refer, of course, to women. Since the early 1970s, the number of women gaining high-level posts and high-level salaries has been steadily increasing, but progress is still very slow. There is no logical or physiological reason why a woman should not run a major international company, but there are a number of psychological reasons why few succeed in doing so. (Before you pounce on that statement and point out that menstruation is a physiological event, let me say that menstruation itself creates no problems that cannot be alleviated medically. It is the mood-change effect it has on us and the mystique surrounding it that creates the problems – and these both come under the psychological heading.)

The real problem areas are the way men see us and themselves, the way we see them and ourselves, and the interlocking relationships between the two. I dislike the militancy invoked by some feminists, but it has to be said that if we women want our share of opportunity, we must fight for it. To fight effectively, we must first recognise the enemy, and in a business setting that enemy is three-fold. The first part is the *company* – its history, structure and attitudes. The second part is the *men* – either the men who surround you in the office or the men in your private life.

The third, and by far the biggest, is *yourself* – your self-respect, self-image, self-confidence, your vision of what you want from life, and your desire and determination to attain it. Many of us are our own worst enemy in this respect.

If you want to climb the business management ladder there is nothing to stop you except your own inability to recognise and defeat or avoid these enemies. The purpose of this book is to enable you to recognise and understand them, and to help you draw up your battle-plan by giving you the basics of career planning, time management, home life management and the management of relationships with your superiors, your peers and your staff.

1 What is a manager?

'Manager' and 'executive' are more or less interchangeable words used today to describe the people who run large organisations. The dictionary definitions are 'designed or fitted to execute or perform, concerned with performance, administration or management' (executive) and 'one who manages; a person who controls a business or other concern; one who organises other people's doings' (manager).

Management, therefore, is the art of getting things done. Not of doing them yourself, but of getting them done by other people. The sheer size of most organisations prevents the people in charge from being able to do things themselves. They just don't have the time to do all the necessary jobs and must employ staff to do them instead. The normal set-up is like a pyramid, with the managing director at the top, a layer of directors or senior managers below him, then layers of middle managers, junior managers, assistant managers, supervisors, and finally a wide assortment of clerks, typists, estimators and so on at the bottom.

The interesting thing about all this is that the amount of technical specialisation needed reduces as you climb the pyramid. Taking a civil engineering company as an example, the estimators need to know the price of a ton of cement and how many tons are needed for a mile of motorway, or how many shovels will be needed, lost or broken in the process of laying that cement. The manager of the estimating department needs to have a rough idea of these figures, to ensure that the estimates produced by his staff are correct, but he does not need to check each item in the latest shovel catalogue. What he does need to be able to do is ensure that all the parts of a complex pricing job will be completed and typed in time for *his* boss to check it, add a profit margin figure to cover overheads and submit the tender in the form needed within the given time limit. The managing director does not need to know any of the fine details, but he does need to know how much the whole job will cost from week to week, because he has to consider whether the company can afford to pay the workers and cement suppliers from their own money until such time as they are paid for doing the job.

And since 'their own money' usually means borrowed money these days, he has to take into consideration such details as interest rates, possible political changes which could affect these rates, the temper of their bankers, insurers and workforce. All these details will come from other sides of the pyramid – accountants, economists, insurance department and union negotiators. (The cynical may suggest that he should also be on good social terms with the Minister of Transport.)

So the managing director's speciality is the ability to juggle all the factors needed for an accurate overview – and this is where we come in. There is as much satisfaction to be gained from completing a major business project as there is in creating a perfectly typed report, a good dinner or a beautiful piece of embroidery. Men have known this for years, but women are only just beginning to realise it. And far from management being the stressful job of popular belief, a recent report proved that heart attacks were twice as likely among foremen and shop-floor workers as among senior executives, with the rate dropping consistently as the ladder ascended. A secretary often suffers from more stress than her boss.

Running a business or a department, doing it right and getting results is *fun*. It is failing to get the right results, or being prevented from taking responsibility, that brings frustrations and stress-related diseases. Which is not to say that being a manager means only doing the jobs you like. Far from it. There are many distasteful tasks which fall to managers, from reprimanding sloppy staff to negotiating with difficult suppliers or placating irate customers.

It is these unpleasant tasks that need the toughness traditionally ascribed to men and which women are supposed to lack. If we do, or if we exhibit the outward signs of softness, it is mostly the fault of our upbringing.

Little boys are encouraged to take risks and to explore the boundaries of courage. Little girls are not. A boy who falls out of a tree, or off his bike, or comes home bruised and bleeding from a scrap, might be scolded by his mother for tearing his clothes, but will recognise the 'boys will be boys' tone in her voice. His father will almost certainly react with pride at the attempt and actively encourage another try by discussing or demonstrating better techniques. Thus encouraged, the average boy tries again until he has succeeded, or at least improved his performance to a level where he can be satisfied with it. He learns at an early age that risks offer chances of improvement.

A girl who tries the same activities will usually find her efforts met with totally negative reactions. Not only might she get hurt, she will certainly get dirty – and it is soon made clear to her that neither is desirable. Worse than that, she will soon realise that both her parents (and most other little girls) will think she is odd – and if there is one thing all children dislike, it is to be considered strange.

Far from the 'nice try–better luck next time' her brother receives for taking a risk, she soon learns that such behaviour is considered aberrant. It is hardly surprising that, faced with these responses, most girls learn to reject any form of risk-taking as leading to totally negative results.

But why? We know that human females are actually physiologically more robust than males. The statistical chances of a female surviving birth and its first year of life are much higher than for a male. Any life assurance company will tell you that females live longer than males now that the worst hazards of childbirth are medically controllable.

So what is all this stuff about big strong men and weak little women? Sheer survival, that's what – and to understand why, you have to go back a few million years to the dawn of humanity. The price of human brain power is the length of time it takes to grow from birth to physical and mental maturity. Our young spend many years in a weak and vulnerable condition and for them to survive at all means constant care. Mature females, like female animals, would have been pregnant or nursing on an almost permanent basis, so could not contribute much to the hunt or long-distance foraging expeditions. It is hardly surprising then that they remained close to the tribal base, looking after the children and doing as much foraging as they could with a babe in arms and a toddler hanging on wherever it could get a grip. (That has to be why we invented skirts – can you imagine a two-year-old hanging on to your leg-fur all day?)

That left the men free to go off hunting, but we needed something to make sure they came back again with the spoils. Evolution provided part of the incentive by making us sexually receptive throughout the year rather than during a brief season. The rest of it came from the female recognition that what a chap wants after a hard day at the mammoth hunt is to come home to a nice receptive biddable woman who will soothe his hurts and tell him what a fine fellow he is.

They may not have been pretty by our standards, those

Australopithecine ladies, but they were no fools. Faced with the choice between risking their own hides pursuing bad-tempered beasts, or staying at home in a nice cosy cave with a fire between them and the long-toothed nasties outside, they chose the latter. All it cost was a bit of independence and some acquiescent behaviour.

But we don't have to do that stuff any more, do we? Meat comes in neat plastic packs in the supermarket and we can choose not to have a parcel of kids round our necks if we don't want them. We are free to leave the cave and earn our living for ourselves, rather than second-hand through our mate. And there is the crux of the matter – earning a living, not just a little pin-money. All the time our ambitions stayed at the level of low-paid subservient jobs there were no problems. Men saw us in the support roles they thought were our natural place, employers enjoyed a cheap labour force and we were convinced we were fulfilling our feminine needs by making a little money in a non-threatening, non-competitive way.

Except that more and more of us looked at the men we worked with and thought, 'If that idiot can do that job, so can I. Why am I sitting here on a third of his salary?' There are two answers to that one. The first is that it has never occurred to anyone that you might want a 'male' job, of which more later. The second is that you don't have the image of a manager – and the sad fact of the matter is that you are not going to be taken seriously until you do acquire that image.

The image you want is one of authority. There was a time when the mere fact that you had the title 'boss' meant you were obeyed. All you had to say was 'You're fired', and the offending member of staff was out of a job. Try it these days and you'll make yourself unpopular with the Personnel department for giving them all the hassle of coping with an industrial tribunal. The big stick no longer exists, so if you want to get your staff to obey you, you have to rely on the fact that people who look and behave as though they expect to be obeyed usually are.

It takes a pretty rare and deliberately rebellious person actively to refuse to obey authority. Both instinct and many generations of acquired behaviour patterns have conditioned us to do as we are told.

Any animal whose survival depends on the survival of the group (pack, herd or tribe) develops a hierarchy of command, and any member of that group who behaves in a way that jeopardises the survival of the group is rapidly disciplined by his superiors or ejected from the group to fend for himself. Humans are no exception to this rule, especially since we are sociable hunting animals. We are not equipped with the weight, claws or teeth to kill large prey on our own, so if we want enough meat to feed the non-hunting members of the tribe as well as the hunters, we must form hunting units. Each member will have his job to do and if he fails to do it, the hunt will fail. At best the prey will escape and everyone goes hungry. At worst, if our errant friend does something really stupid when the prey is big and dangerous, he could get himself and others killed.

It is natural that the wisest member of the band should be the one to assume the lead and tell the others what to do. One of the perks of the job is first pick of the meat, which results in his being better fed, stronger and probably bigger than the rest. Because of the perks, vacancies for the job will be hotly contested and if the contest is settled by a fight it is likely to be won by the biggest and strongest contender. And that size and strength is what helps to keep the others in line and obedient.

In the history of mankind, it is only in the last couple of centuries that power has been enforced economically rather than physically. Power and size have become synonymous in our instincts. And that presents us with a problem, for most of us are smaller than most men. There is little we can do about this physically, although I suppose one could arrange for all one's staff to be smaller by selective interviewing, but there are some ploys we can use to make us look bigger than we actually are.

Higher heels may be your first thought, but they must not be so high that they are difficult to walk on. Teetering around reduces you to the sex object level: just think of the history of keeping women subjugated by restricting their movement, from the practice of deforming feet by binding, to declaring it immodest to sit astride a horse.

You can use your hairstyle to give you extra height and your clothes to give you bulk if you are particularly tiny. Big lapels and padded shoulders are helpful, for they emulate the threat display used by almost all mammals, where the head is dropped and the shoulders and back are raised. In really difficult situations with subordinates it is useful physically to do this yourself. Take a deep breath and hold it as long as you can to raise your diaphragm (and your facial colour – another warning of trouble), round your shoulders up and forward and thrust your chin out – and watch your opponent pull himself up and back. Don't try it with a male boss. He may be annoyed and react by advancing on you so *you* have to back off.

Part of this has to do with what is called 'acceptance distance' – the amount of space you need between you and the other person to feel comfortable. The general rule is that the better you know, or want to know, the other person, the smaller your acceptance distance. Lovers stand or sit much closer than friends, acquaintances are allowed much nearer than strangers.

Superiors feel they are entitled to encroach on subordinates' space, but not vice versa. A lot of men will do this to women and it puts you at a double disadvantage, partly because they are too close and partly because that very closeness means that to look at their eyes you have to adopt the supplicating position of putting your head back to look up at them, or you have to step back – in other words, retreat.

If anybody does this to you consistently, you can be reasonably sure it is deliberate and prevent it by moving in closer yourself until they have to step back to preserve their own distance. If you dare, emphasise what you are saying by using hand gestures that further infringe their space. If all else fails, apply the subtle female put-down of picking imaginary lint off their clothes ('Just stand still, dear, while I tidy you up') but *don't ever* adjust his tie. A tie is a penis symbol and if you handle it, he'll get the wrong idea!

The alternative is to avoid such situations by meeting on your own ground. If you have your own office it is quite easy to organise it to give you additional advantages. Everyone knows you should sit with your back to the window so visitors have to squint into the light, but there are lots of other power-ploys you can use.

The main one is that you maximise your space and minimise theirs, by bringing your desk away from the window to leave lots of room behind you and none for them. If you can arrange it so they have to squeeze in behind a door, so much the better. Just be careful the arrangement does not allow them to move their chair round to your side of the desk and impinge on your space.

Go for the biggest desk you can. This keeps you aloof by increasing the distance between you and visitors and has the added advantage of allowing perspective to make them look smaller to you. The only snag is that it might make you look smaller too, so the desk should be deep rather than wide. Don't let the furniture people give you an enormous chair that dwarfs you. Do get them to provide lower chairs for visitors or, best of all, soft ones they sink into.

Beware the visitor who takes over your space by moving his things over your desk towards you. Either preempt this by keeping your desk so full he has no room to put anything, or pick up his stuff to look at and put it down close to you, thus claiming it as your own.

And of course, when you have to go to someone else's office, keep all these things in mind and utilise them to your own advantage. Select the chair you sit in and move it to where you want to be, not where they put you. If there isn't a suitable chair, plead a back injury and make them get you one. Make yourself some desk space and generally behave as if you have a right to be there, rather than as a supplicant.

Don't *ever* behave like a supplicant. You have every right to be in your job and to ask for whatever you need to do it better, whether that is a training course to increase your knowledge, adequate performance from your staff, or a promotion that will allow you to make a bigger contribution to the company's success. All predators look for easy prey, from the wolf looking for an injured moose to the mugger looking for a scuttling nervous victim, or the office sexual pest or one of your peers hoping to beat you to a promotion. If you behave like a timid little creature you will be treated like one, and your superiors will certainly not think of you as promotion material.

Even if it is only observed subconsciously, body language reveals an awful lot about you. Women are brought up to behave submissively, looking down to avoid eye contact, standing or sitting in ways that make us appear small, and smiling a lot to placate the dominant male. We adjust our behaviour to the initiatives of others (stepping back when they advance, instead of standing our ground or advancing on them) and we tend to fidget when we are nervous, or make small grooming gestures like tucking in loose strands of hair.

To make people believe you are in control of yourself and do not consider yourself to be inferior, you must adopt an upright balanced position, whether sitting or standing, which means with your weight evenly distributed on both feet or buttocks. I still cringe at the memory of the time I perched on one buttock on my desk, for the benefit of a gorgeous hunk of male visitor, only to find that I was sitting on a nerve which made me shudder uncontrollably while the brute laughed at me.

If you are not balanced you will not be able to sit still comfortably, and you will not be able to relax. If you cross your legs, you will probably want to uncross and/or recross them, with the risk of your audience assuming you are flashing your thighs at them. So – sit up, sit still, keep your hands still, maintain a steady confident eye contact and keep the ingratiating smile off your face. Especially avoid tilting your head when you smile – it is one of the 'come on' signals.

Remember that less than 10 per cent of the message is in the words you use. Over half is in the way you look when you say them, and the rest is in the way you actually deliver them. Many women have a tendency to apologise every time they speak, without intending to. They either use phrases like 'Would you mind if . . .' or 'I'm afraid I haven't been able to . . .' or they turn their statements into questions by a rising inflection at the end. Then they add that ingratiating smile to minimise the impertinence of speaking at all.

Do you do it? What the hell for? Questions are for finding out facts you need to know. Apologising is for when you've done something wrong, not for merely existing. If you've got something to say, say it firmly but quietly. Don't get loud – female loud usually comes out shrill and that is no help at all.

If you haven't got anything constructive to say, don't. Even in a one-to-one situation, just keep quiet, maintain that confident eye contact and wait. Many people become acutely embarrassed by long silences and will babble to fill the gap. You are likely to hear the most interesting and useful things and you will have enhanced your reputation as a cool, confident lady. And that, careerwise, is the most useful reputation you can get.

2 Career planning

Many of the women in senior management posts today tell a similar story of their start on the management ladder. They spent the first twelve or fifteen years of their working life in a series of subordinate jobs, waiting for Prince Charming to come along and carry them off to live happily ever after. When he didn't turn up, or after he'd let them down, they realised they were going to have to support themselves for the rest of their lives. Close on that realisation came another – that they needed a better salary or a better challenge – and so they promptly set about achieving both.

Most of these women started work when it was unusual to encounter women in commerce in any situation other than behind a typewriter, and when marrying meant stopping work. Although that time has long gone, the number of women who realise at thirty-five that they need a decent career has increased tremendously. The divorce rate has gone up and most women still get custody of their children. Socio-economic expectations have risen, and you can no longer put your children through university, nor maintain a civilised lifestyle, on a secretary's salary.

Even with a stable marriage, many women are realising the waste of their abilities and seeking a senior position. Younger women are also looking for a long-term career. Unfortunately few of them get very far, for they have not grasped the essential fact. *You must plan your career.*

It really is no good sitting at your desk all frustrated, complaining to yourself that 'I could do better than this' – unless, of course, you get your jollies out of doing just that. There is a newish theory of psychology called 'transactional analysis' that says we view ourselves and those around us in an 'OK/not OK' light and that we spend our lives playing a series of 'games' made up of variations of 'OK/not OK'.

The games that concern us here are the ones we play in a career situation. There's 'Wouldn't It Be Nice If' (I had a better job), 'Gee Ain't It Awful' (my boss is incompetent and I could do his job standing on my head), and 'Somebody Oughta Do Something' (about providing some training and jobs for women like me), all of which mean 'I'm OK, they're not OK'. And then there's 'Poor Little Me' (I'd love to be a manager but I don't think I could cope with the responsibility and stress) or 'My Husband Wouldn't Like It' (or at least I don't think he would, although I haven't dared mention it to him), which both translate as 'They're OK, I'm not OK.'

Here's a new one for you. 'They're OK, I'm OK – but not as OK as I could be' or 'They're all getting on with their jobs and their lives, I'm intelligent, competent and possessed of ability, but I could be in a better job so I'd best see how to go about getting one.'

Which brings us back to where we started. You must plan how to achieve your ambition, just as you must plan a journey. Which presupposes that you know where you want to get to. If you do, you are lucky, for your destination is clear and all you need to do is work out how to get there.

If all you have is frustration, boredom, a low salary and a sense of your life wasting away, your first task is some fundamental self-analysis. You could go to a vocational guidance agency, but you must be sure they are interested in more than just your fee. Some also act as employment agencies (not a good idea, it means you are actually paying them to find you a job), some are biased towards particular professions, and some have neither women consultants nor sympathy towards women. (I have not yet cooled down from the one I encountered who told me of all the 'girls' he had found jobs for. He was not amused when I called him a 'boy'!) Others do an excellent job, with a full range of services from counselling and CV production to mock interviews on video to help you polish your performance.

But they are expensive. If you don't want to spend several hundred pounds, lock yourself in your bedroom for a couple of hours with pen and paper and ask yourself these questions. What am I good at? What am I bad at? What could I be better at if I tried and what do I dislike so much I don't want to do it at all? List all the thoughts that come to you, including the domestic items like arranging dinner parties. Are you articulate, happy to speak in front of a group, good at organising other people into a team – or are you happier working on your own? It is all relevant. When the flow has stopped, back off from the answers a bit and see if you can detect a trend.

If you hate writing letters and always got low marks for essays at school, but keep a neat bank book, you could consider the accountancy route to the top. Add to it the ability to organise a big dinner party and keep records of everybody's likes and dislikes and you'll be a good enough organiser to make a company secretary. The opposite – hate figures, love writing, love people – maybe you should go for Personnel or Marketing.

Have you had a series of jobs in one industry? Do you secretly hate it and want to do something completely different? Do you want to utilise your experience and stay in it, or do you secretly hanker for a job on the board of your present company?

If after all this you still don't know what you want to do, it might be worth while giving up your present job and temping for a year. All employment agencies welcome temps with open arms, and they don't just want secretaries. They get a regular income from you as opposed to a one-off fee when they find you a permanent job. Tell them you want to work in a variety of companies, put up with the inconvenience of travelling all over the place and wait to see if any of the industries you encounter strike any chords.

At the same time, do some study or attend evening classes in a general business discipline. Then your CV won't look as though you were fired, as you can explain that you wanted a non-demanding job while you were studying. How flattering, too, to tell a prospective employer, 'I wasn't sure what I wanted to do, so I tried all sorts of things until I knew it was to work for you.'

Once you have worked out which ladder you want to climb, you can consider the route and the equipment you need to help you in your ascent. Start by looking at some of the people at the top now and find out how they got there. Unless they have stepped into Daddy's shoes, they will almost certainly have had several changes of company on the way up. The exceptions are such industries as banking, where experience is gained by moving from branch to branch in a clearly laid-down progression. If you have not chosen such an industry, you must also be prepared to build such moves into your plan.

There is a fair chance that your first move may need to be to a lower rung on another ladder, with a lower salary while you learn the job, so your first task must be to acquire a financial buffer. If you are already living in a bed-sitter, eating nothing but bread and cheese, and walking to work, you'd better give up your job and return to full-time study on a grant. If not, you have just come to the first of the 'taking control of my life' decisions – are you prepared to pay the price of turning your dream to reality?

Are you willing to give up your holiday abroad, or wait

another year for new carpets? Do you really need your own car? Can you live without nail-polish, perfume and your weekly visit to the hairdresser? The more you are prepared to sacrifice now, the sooner you'll have the necessary buffer in the bank to tide you over a couple of lean years and the sooner you will get high enough on your new ladder to reap the benefits of seniority.

The next nasty pricing question is: are you prepared to invest your leisure time and brainpower in the future? If you already have a degree or a professional qualification you may need to add another (Diploma in Management Studies, MBA or MSc, for instance) or get some training in a modern discipline like Computer Studies. If you lack the required professional qualification for your chosen industry, you will need to get it. Either will take a minimum of two evenings a week for up to four years.

If you have no qualifications at all, you will have to acquire some. Valuable though common sense is, you can't list it on your CV. When every job is hotly contested by fully qualified but unemployed candidates, submitting a bald CV will get you weeded out before the first interview. Studying the advertisements for jobs you'd like will tell you what qualifications you need. Your local library will guide you towards finding out how and where to study.

If you are still at the 'don't know what I want to do' stage, start off by doing a National Certificate (or Diploma) in Business Studies. You don't necessarily even need GCEs to start, though they do like them, but you can get some as you go along with little extra effort, since the GCE syllabus is very close in content to most of the subjects involved. The courses take two years, look good on your CV, and may even give you exemption from the first year of your chosen professional exams.

Good general qualifications, for any industry, are in

accountancy (especially management accounts), company secretaryship, taxation or law. Even without the actual end result, most employers are impressed by your commitment. Larger companies will actively encourage you by paying your professional membership fee, tuition and exam fees, and give you extra 'study' leave before you sit the exams.

The final 'price' question relates to your personal life on a more permanent basis than the few years needed to get some letters after your name. I will be covering the whole areas of home, husband and children in detail later, but you need to consider them when choosing your route. Small children and a job that involves a lot of travelling are not a good combination, nor are twelve- to sixteen-year-olds and the need to relocate to the other end of the country. Some careers, such as accountancy, will not suffer if you take a few years' break for breeding, whereas other careers will be destroyed completely if you do it at the wrong time.

A husband in a solid job with a good salary allows you to take risks that you could not if he were a self-employed salesman with an erratic income. A husband who travels a lot usually wants to be welcomed home to recover quietly between trips. If you don't provide what he needs, he may think of replacing you. On the other hand, you may be thinking of replacing him, in which case devoting yourself heavily to your career advancement for a couple of years is an excellent way of alleviating the trauma of separation and divorce.

Some final thoughts on choice of career. Do think carefully about economic trends, so you don't waste time and effort by specialising in an area which has a short-term future. This is known in America as the 'buggy-whip syndrome'. But don't make the mistake of getting over-involved in modern technology either – computer-programming, on its own, is not a good route to the board-room.

If you do have your eye on a seat on the board, beware of what are called 'cul-de-sac' careers. These are the ones with a low promotion ceiling, like Office Services or Personnel. Yes, I know personnel managers have to be highly qualified and can be well paid in big companies, and that it is one of the 'caring' professions considered suitable for women – but it ain't gonna put you up there among the *real* decision-makers.

Whichever route you choose isn't going to take you there overnight, either. It takes anything from fifteen to twenty-five years to get from junior manager to top executive level, with changes of job every three or four years. Each change should bring another aspect of experience to act as a stepping-stone, and each change should be built into your plan.

Do you find it alarming to contemplate planning the next two decades? It does not have to be a rigid plan, mapped out week by week for the rest of your working life, but it does need to have the next couple of moves sketched in, with some alternatives thought out in case of need. Otherwise you may find the move you make now will be the wrong one.

Men, who have grown up knowing they have to work all their lives, do it as a matter of course, which is why they succeed. If you do not do the same, you will spend the rest of your life drifting unhappily from job to job. No one else is going to do it for you. You have to realise that the pattern of your life is in your own hands and accept the responsibility for controlling it. The managing director is not going to spot your talent as you sit behind your typewriter and carry you off on his white charger to the executive suite, but he might choose you above other job applicants if your CV shows the right experience.

Even the best planned route may turn out to lead to an

unforeseeable dead end. The company may be taken over, or have a major change of policy that leaves you out on a limb, or your supportive boss may move on where you cannot follow, to be replaced by someone you cannot tolerate. The boss you've attached yourself to may turn out to be an also-ran instead of the winner you expected, or he may get a new boss who blocks his progress.

Abandon any day dreams you may have about your incompetent boss being fired and yourself stepping into his shoes. It rarely happens like that. The more usual scenario is that he will be replaced by someone who will want his own chosen team under him. You are more likely to be tainted with the old boss's reputation of incompetence or, worse, if you have been rash enough to voice your opinion of him, as disloyal. The only sensible step you can take when working under an incompetent is to step away from him – either into another department or another company.

If your job has become routine and there is no obvious next step, if you have reached a salary ceiling, if the company won't help you with training, or if you've been in your present job so long you are regarded as a permanent fixture, you've reached a dead end. Don't assume that the company's concept of what it wants from you is compatible with what you need from it.

Forget all that loyalist stuff about not leaving your boss in the lurch. He wouldn't give it a thought if his career was at stake, and neither should you. Your first duty is to yourself and your own career development. If you can't get what you need from the situation you're in, you must make up your mind to go and find it somewhere else.

It may be that your best opportunity for advancement is to work for a small or growing company. If you are the only woman, or one in a minority, you will certainly have high visibility and real chances of getting close to the top echelons. The snags in such companies are that the salary levels tend to be lower, and promotion and salary review procedures may not be formalised, but there is less competition for any promotion opportunities which do occur.

Consider starting with a small company and moving to a larger one when you have acquired some experience and seniority. Larger companies are less likely to consider a woman in management as a novelty, but more likely to be heavily political. More about office politics later. You may not like them, but they are a fact of office life and cannot be ignored.

The best base for job-hunting is from secure employment, for it proves someone finds you employable. It also takes some of the heat out of the need to find a job – any job – which may lead to rash decisions. No matter how ghastly your current job is, stick with it until you have another job offer in writing.

Don't ever resign in anger. It might make you feel better at the time, but the reverberations will linger on. It could influence the reference they give you and, anyway, Murphy's Law says someone in the new company you join will know your old boss. They're bound to mention you to him and you don't want him to tell them you have a bad temper.

Beware also of threatening to resign if the company doesn't give you what you want. The chance that they will is far less than the likelihood that they will welcome the opportunity of getting rid of a prima donna so painlessly.

When you have accepted a new job, do resign gracefully. Sound regretful at leaving, but explain that you have been offered a challenge/salary you can't turn down. They may respond with a better offer, but even if they don't, you might want to go back to them in the future.

'Career progression' is really the only acceptable answer to a prospective new employer who asks why you want to change. Just wanting more money is not, for it implies your current bosses do not consider you are worth any more, and 'personality conflict' implies that *you* are difficult to get on with. The worst excuse of all is that hoary old stand-by 'redundancy'. Unless the whole company or a large division has gone under, the implication is invariably that the term is a face-saver when you have been sacked for incompetence or trouble-making. Indeed, with today's employment laws making it difficult to get rid of entrenched staff, declaring you redundant is the cheapest and easiest way for any company to 'let you go'. Many firms of professional headhunters consider redundancy to be an incurable disease and will not take anybody with that taint.

The best way to start looking for a new job is through your friends and business contacts. Talk to them about opportunities in their company and let them know you might think of moving if the right offer were made. Don't be negative about your present employers – emphasise your own plus points instead. If they believe you, your contacts will be only too willing to tell their bosses about you. Think how much good it will do them to have been instrumental in your recruitment.

For this reason alone it is worth maintaining your visibility outside your company. Attend meetings of the local branch of your professional body; write articles for, or letters to, your industry's trade magazines; do everything you can to make people aware that you exist and know your stuff.

If you are not already a member of any of the women's networks (see the Appendix) join whichever seem appropriate to your situation and ambitions. They exist to provide contacts and support and many of them also offer all kinds of self-development courses. The general attitude I have encountered in them is, 'We may have got where we are on our own, but we don't see why you should have such a struggle when we are here to help.'

If nothing comes from your own contacts, the next step is to register with some agencies. Start with PER*, add the agencies that specialise in the industry that particularly interests you and some specialist 'executive' placement agencies. Forget the rest – most of them only deal with clerks and secretaries. Just remember that they are not working for you but for the companies with vacancies to fill. That is where their fees come from and it is a rare agency that will take the trouble to find a square hole for a square peg. If you have the requisite qualifications to fit any of the round holes on their list, fine. If not, they will probably do no more than send you their vacancy list, file your CV away and forget you.

A technique that has worked well for me in the past is to select a likely company and write to them, saying something on the lines of, 'I am impressed with what I know of you. I would like to work for you. I believe I can contribute to your future success. Here's my CV – can I come and talk to you?'

Don't send it to the Personnel department, send it to the managing director. Although he will inevitably pass it to Personnel to deal with, it will carry some urgency with it since it has come from him and they know he will expect a report on you.

If one avenue of job-hunting doesn't work, try another. Whilst the personal contact or agency method are undoubtedly the best, there is nothing wrong with answering advertisements. But do read them carefully before writing. It is no good applying for a job that specifies a

*Professional and Executive Register is run by the Manpower Services Commission and will send you their weekly jobs newspaper, *Executive Post*, indefinitely. They are at Fitzwilliam House, Fitzwilliam Gate, Sheffield S1 4JH.

professional qualification you do not have. On the other hand, if you have five of the six requirements stated, don't assume you won't be considered. Many men with three would apply on the basis that the plus points they have will offset the ones they don't. Anyway, many job specifications are written by the actual job-holder, who is bound to assume that his job can only be done by another identical person. If you appear to be that desirable an employee, they might be prepared to juggle the job content to accommodate your talents.

Always send a covering letter with your CV and mention the annual salary range you want, not how much you are getting now. Keep a list of starting and finishing salaries of your previous jobs – they always ask on application forms – but don't put them on your CV.

All management-level job applications should be accompanied by your CV, whether they ask for it or not, so be sure it works properly for you, listing all your achievements, abilities and strengths as well as qualifications and job experience. One superb one I saw started off: 'Broad summary – through the medium of international work experience I have a proven dedication to accept challenge and objectively tackle projects requiring both specific and interdisciplinary skills, initiate and implement new concepts and projects; communicate and negotiate at a senior level; manage and supervise supportive staff.'

It's not what you've done, it's how you put it. Remember, this is a selling aid and it must catch the customer's eye and make them want to know more. Don't put 'secretary to marketing manager, duties included fact-finding, typing letters and reports and filing' when you could put 'development of corporate promotional literature, establishment of office procedures'.

It doesn't matter too much what order the facts are in,

whether you start with education and qualifications or put them at the end; or whether you start job details with the job you have now or the first job you ever had. But do be sure there are no unexplained gaps in your job history – suspicious personnel officers might wonder if you were in prison!

Keep the personal details sparse – for instance: 'British citizen. Born 1950, divorced, no children, interested in opera, horse-riding and tennis.' If you have ever had any articles published, or presented papers to conferences, list them.

List any other experience and skills you may have acquired in non-work areas that will demonstrate your management ability. Mine, for instance, says: 'Formed Ladies' Side-Saddle Association and served as Chairman for six years, overseeing formation of affiliated international groups, negotiating with sponsors and event organisers. Has travelled extensively in Europe, Canada and the USA to lecture and appear on TV. Has published numerous articles and five books. Lectures on Time and Money Management and Writing Skills.' Most of that refers to my horsey activities, but it proves I can start and run a complex organisation, communicate at all levels, that I am not afraid to speak my piece in front of an audience, and that I can express myself on paper – all good management skills. You may have similar plus points to list, even if it is no more than running a Girl Guide group – but even that requires leadership skills and you should emphasise them.

Finally, do not forget to list all the trips you have been on for your employers and any courses or conventions they've sent you to. These have added to your skills, and it also proves your employers thought you were worth the expense.

If you do not feel you can do an adequate job on your CV yourself, there are agencies that will do it for you after a fact-finding interview (they advertise in the daily papers). Considering the professional job they produce, their fee is not exorbitant, especially if you regard it as another investment in your future.

Once your CV has done its preliminary work and got you an interview, you have another task to attend to – and that is to find out all you can about the company concerned. When discussing interview times on the telephone, ask them to send you copies of their annual report for the last few years. Not only will they not be surprised, they will mark it down as a point in your favour. Check them out in the library, in the financial papers and with your business acquaintances. Try to form a picture of them before you get to the interview and it will help you know how to comport yourself. They may, for instance, have a heavy religious leaning, in which case you would be unwise to state that you are an atheist or mention that your live-in lover has not bothered to get a divorce.

If it is your first attempt at a management job, remember when you get to the interview that executives are supposed to be able to cope with pressure and be at your calmest and most self-confident. Emphasise your positive points, your ability to accept responsibility and to get results, your dependability, willingness to learn and general co-operativeness, but particularly your achievements related to cutting costs and increasing profits, for management is extensively concerned with money.

When the interviewer asks if you have any questions, emphasise your commitment to a long-term career by asking detailed questions about the company itself. He or she will be able to tell you far more about the potential of the company in general, and as a vehicle for your ambitions in particular, than all your research. But without that research, you won't know what questions to ask. Serious managers want to work for companies that are profitable and have growth potential – in other words, winners.

Ask how many people have held the job in question and for how long, and abandon the idea if the answer is more than two in the last five years. Remember the old saying – 'once is an accident, twice is coincidence, three times is enemy action' – and don't expose yourself to what looks like an impossible situation. Ask about the general turnover rate of executives. Too few and your promotion prospects are limited. Too many and there is a high-level problem that could affect you as well. Ask about the managing director. Is he competent, reasonable, an autocrat or an autocrat's inadequate son? Is he a man with a history of job-hopping? All this will affect the company's future prospects – and yours.

Ask what your position will be on the company ladder and your prospects for advancement. Ask the specific question, 'Do you see any objections to a woman in this job?' and discuss them before you go any further. Don't let the interview ramble off down side-tracks, especially if they are connected with the fact that you are a woman. Keep emphasising the details of the job itself and your commitment to your career. No, your husband does not object to your working long hours – nor do you object to doing so. Yes, you do have a well-organised child-care plan that leaves you free to concentrate on your work. No, you do not intend to have children in the next few years – you don't want it to interfere with your study plans. If you do decide to have children, it is your intention to return to work immediately. And anyway, would they rather lose you to pregnancy or a competitor?

If they like what they've learned, you will normally be invited back for a second interview with someone more senior. This is part of the weeding-out process and nothing to worry about. The wait will give you time to work out whether you are really interested. In the unlikely event that they offer you the job there and then, keep cool and ask for a few days to think about it. It is easy to get carried away with the situation, especially if you have found yourself in a controlling role, and you could find you feel differently about it the next day. It won't hurt to play hard to get. It might even increase the salary. Just don't believe it is in the bag until you get that offer letter.

Although changing companies is often the best, or the only, way to get on to the next rung of your career ladder, or even to get the salary you deserve, don't be tempted to do it too often. Unless you are head-hunted with an offer you can't refuse, you should expect to stay in each job a minimum of two years and preferably more. At one time it was the norm for computer personnel to change jobs at eighteen-month intervals, to gain experience with different machines and different programming languages, but even that volatile industry has changed. Four years is a more acceptable time in most industries.

Too many changes of job make you look unreliable and imply that either you are incapable of settling, or that you make a practice of moving rapidly before your bad reputation catches up with you.

It takes longer for a woman to establish good working relationships with her male peers, and it is not sensible to abandon these and move to another company where you have to start all over again unless there is no alternative. Far better to plan to move sideways and upwards in the company where you are accepted and trusted and where you know who are enemies and who are friends – and how to handle both.

3 Advancement within your present company

Nice girls don't compete, they sit politely and wait to be chosen. Or so my mother told me. Even at an early age, I could never quite reconcile this with 'if you don't ask, you don't get', which was said to us at mealtimes, but it is only in the last few years that I have realised what a problem it creates in a career situation. Generations of women have grown up convinced that if they do their best, they will be noticed and rewarded, then wondered why the rewards were not forthcoming.

The reason is a fundamental one. You can't expect to be given something if people don't know you want it. No matter how competently you get on with your assigned task, no one will know you want a more challenging one if you don't tell them. Promotion does not come from doing a good job, it comes as the incentive for taking on a more important and responsible job. If you don't ask for one, it will be assumed that you are happy as you are.

The problem you have to face is that women are still largely regarded as temporary workers. If you are seen as being in a job only while you wait for marriage or child-birth, or for the length of time it takes to put your children through college, or for some trivial reason like paying for the family holidays, it is hardly surprising that the assumption is that you don't want responsibility or advancement. Or that it isn't worth spending money training you if you aren't going to be around for long.

Unless you work for one of the enlightened companies who have analysed their staff retention figures, or who already have a number of women halfway up the ladder (or maybe even one at the top) you may have to tell them loud and long before they get the message.

It is rarely that they don't want to promote you at all, more that it had never occurred to them that you might be interested. So we come back to taking control of your own life, which in this instance means letting the people who matter know that you are serious about your career.

Start with your own boss. If your company has a formal appraisal system, the review interview is the time to bring up the subject. Say as bluntly as your relationship with your boss allows, 'I want to get on. I want a proper career. My goal is this. What is the best way for me to progress upwards?' And make sure he records both that and his response on your assessment sheet.

If there is no formal system, then make an appointment with him and let him know in advance that you want to discuss your career progression. Don't spring it on him at a time when he can put you off with the excuse, legitimate or otherwise, that he is too busy. If you think he will suppress your ambitions by keeping them to himself, then make sure he cannot by sending him a memo saying: 'You will note that I have booked myself into your diary for an hour on Thursday. The purpose of this meeting is to discuss my career prospects with the company.' And send a copy to Personnel, with that fact marked on the top copy.

Explain your commitment to a proper career and your desire for more challenging duties. Tell him that you are confident of your ability to cope with seniority and anxious to improve your financial position. Give him a minute to take it in, then ask for his advice and help in achieving your ambition. If he makes unbelieving or discouraging noises, just restate your case firmly but in different words, like a scratched record.

One of the classic examples of this is the situation where

your boss affects not to understand why you want the title of manager. He will produce all sorts of arguments on the lines of 'We all know you do the job, so why do you think you need the title?' Or 'We don't go much on titles around here.' Your problem is to persist with your stance that the title is important to you without letting him think you are making a lot of fuss over a trivial issue. It is no good getting annoyed about it – he'll label you aggressive. Nor should you be defensive. Don't get into an 'Ah' . . . 'but' . . . session. That won't convince him and won't do anything for your self-confidence either.

If he responds as you hope he will, expressing pleased surprise at your news and request, lead the conversation on into possible areas you might move into. If you have given careful thought to the tasks you might handle and the way you would tackle them, tell him about them and emphasise your specific abilities in those contexts. Then go away and let him think it over.

There are a dozen reasons why your immediate boss will not do anything for you, from inertia to bloody-mindedness, so if you don't see any results from that interview within a reasonable time, make an appointment with Personnel. Say all the same things to them, except that you can widen your scope to positions outside your current department. Don't make disloyal noises of any sort about your boss – don't winge or complain or be scornful of his abilities. That will not encourage them to burden another person with you. Just state clearly and firmly that you are anxious to improve both yourself and your contribution to the company, but that you do not see how you can without moving into another department.

At this point they will probably ask you where you see yourself. You will spoil your chances of being taken seriously if you do not have your answer ready. Tell them of your strengths and ask if they are aware of any weaknesses you should work on. Ask about training, ask if you need any further qualifications, ask what help the company will give and generally make it clear that you are not prepared to settle for second-best.

If, as a result of all this, you are offered a different job – be it in your department or another – take it. Whether or not it is what you wanted to do, if it is a higher rung than the one you are on, or a lower (but similarly rewarded) rung on a better ladder, take it. If you're afraid you won't be able to do it properly, keep your doubts to yourself, trust the company's judgement of your ability and take it. Even if you know you are going to hate every minute of it, if it is a step in the right direction, take it, grit your teeth and make the best of it for at least a year until you can reasonably move on again. If you don't accept it, whatever it is, all you've done is proved that you didn't really mean what you said.

If no offers are forthcoming, just keep applying for internally advertised vacancies until they give you something better. Or until you get what you want outside. It may be that they just don't see you as promotion material. Perhaps you have an over-close style – a reputation for being pernickety which doesn't fit the broader viewpoint a manager should take.

Start to think and talk about the way your job affects the company. When you have ideas to present, think the whole thing through carefully before putting it down on paper. State your reasons for raising whatever it is – increased productivity, reducing costs, preventing errors or whatever – but keep them brief. Give your suggestions for implementation, mention any problems you anticipate and the solutions to them.

Finally, indicate how much of your time it will take and what priority you want to give it, but put the whole thing in a company rather than a personal context.

Don't be surprised if it disappears without trace. It may have been tried before, conflict with some other plan in the pipeline, or just look as though it will be costly at a time when there is an economy drive. Ask your boss what he thought of it, then wait for another idea to try again.

Don't be too aggrieved if he presents it to higher authority as his own scheme. He has his career advancement to consider and part of his job is to get his subordinates to produce.

Take every opportunity to attend courses to increase your management skills. Anything connected with management accounting techniques is valuable, especially budgeting and cash flow. Never forget that management is concerned primarily with money. Report-writing, leadership skills and project management, problem-solving, staff selection and interviewing techniques are all skills you will need – and if you feel you are getting pushed around too much you should seriously consider taking a course in assertiveness training.

All the time you allow people to take advantage of you, you are confirming the 'quiet little submissive woman' image, not the self-confident, self-controlling managerial image you need. It is not easy to make the transition from the 'I'll let you tread on me and be grateful for any crumbs' position to the 'this is what I am entitled to and this is what I intend to have' position without overdoing it and ending up merely being aggressive. Being assertive makes people respect you, being aggressive just upsets them. The distinction can be a fine one, but assertiveness training courses make you do a lot of role playing until you feel happy about coping with most potential situations.

'Aggressive bitch' is not a tag you need. 'Competent woman with potential' is – and it behoves you to be sure it is the one people in high places apply to you. In the same way that nobody is going to know what you want until you tell them, nobody is going to notice you unless you constantly come to their attention – the right way. It's called 'visibility', and it means that you must always be on the look-out for opportunities to bring yourself to the attention of the people who matter. People who do nothing but routine jobs tend to be invisible, so you will need to find something special to do at intervals. Make a point of sitting at the front of meetings and don't be afraid to speak up if you have something to say. Don't wait too long to do it – there is a theory that says if you don't speak during the first ten minutes, you won't speak at all.

Make sure your name appears on as many memos, reports and circulation lists as possible, even if it is only as final recipient for filing. Write letters to the major national daily papers (the *Guardian*, *Telegraph*, *Times* and *Financial Times*) whenever you see an opportunity. Volunteer to take items to the managing director when he calls for them, and if you are able to get past his secretary make sure he actually looks at you by addressing some remark to him. Try to get your photograph in the company magazine. It doesn't really matter what for, as long as it's there.

You never know who might be looking at you, so always turn yourself out immaculately and always be on your best behaviour. No adjusting your tights in the corridor and no giggling after a boozy lunch. Come to think of it, no boozy lunches at all. There are still plenty of people who consider it unladylike to drink, and it impairs your ability to work and make sensible decisions in the afternoon.

There are also plenty of people who know that powerful people are usually beautifully dressed. This is because a major perk of being in charge is that your goodwill is valuable to those around you and they will go out of their way to keep you happy. In primitive times this often took the form of grooming and this, added to the fact that the leader and his family were sleekest because they were best fed, meant that leaders were not only big and strong, they were well turned out, too, and in the past their clothes tended to be of a style that actually made them look bigger.

You could always tell who was Queen, she was the one in the beautiful robes with a jewelled crown. She sat on a throne, too, or its equivalent, and it tended to be up on a platform which put her above the others and made her look bigger still. That is also worth remembering.

So the trappings of power have become equated with power itself in our minds. If you want to be taken seriously as a potential boss, you must learn to look and behave as if you are one, not as a female in a support role. Failure to do this is the single biggest mistake made by women seeking a management career. Make no mistake about it, you are trying to sell your skills in a competitive market place and, as with any other item for sale, packaging counts.

So what should you wear? That is something I can't tell you in precise detail here – it would take a whole book to cover all the permutations of your size, shape and colour and of the type of business you are in, but I can give you some general guidelines. Most importantly, you must remember that you are trying to achieve a competent businesslike managerial image, not a feminine frivolous sexy one. This means you must avoid frills, low necks, bare arms, overtight items, very pale colours and any extremes of high fashion.

The fashion trade wants you to look sexy and it wants you to spend money on fads. Don't do either – go for classic lines which will allow you to build up a substantial wardrobe of good quality clothes that will last for years, rather than items which you won't want to wear next season.

Spending £150 on a dress which is made of good fabric, with generous seams and a full lining makes more sense than spending the same amount on five £30 dresses. The latter will be skimpily cut, badly finished and will need constant ironing and attention to keep them wearable at all. The expensive dress will not need this much attention and you will be able to wear it for many years.

Don't buy clothes on impulse and don't buy them at sales, unless they are genuine 'last season's stock clearance' items from your chosen favourite manufacturer. Do find manufacturers who cut their clothes in a way that fits your backside and shoulders and stick with them. Apart from considerations of fit, they tend to run along their own design style year after year, and each season's items should blend in with previous seasons'.

Do take the time to plan your wardrobe. If necessary, get help. There are independent specialists who will come to your home and assess your existing wardrobe, then help you draw up a plan and even go with you on shopping expeditions, all for an hourly rate. (It's called 'wardrobe engineering' in the USA.) Look for their advertisements in the better monthly magazines.

If all this sounds horrendously expensive, don't despair. I will not deny that to *start* the sort of wardrobe you need to look successful is going to cost a lot of money, but once you have the right basis, it is relatively inexpensive to maintain.

If all else fails and your budget really won't run to good new clothes, go to a good second-hand clothes shop. They are springing up all over the place now, and good clothes can be had for a fraction of the new price. It might be an idea to go to one a little way from your home or office, if you don't want to be seen. If there are none near you, make a trip to London where there are several very reputable and long-established ones (they are in the Yellow Pages under 'Dress

Agencies'). You may be lucky, as I was, in finding one that had regular batches of clothes brought in by a lady who was my size, shape and colouring – and who clearly had more money than sense, for she would buy several identical dresses in different colours and then never wear them. I had several items with the shop tags still in them, all for about a tenth of their original price.

The final questions you must learn to ask yourself before you buy *anything* are: How much is it? How long will it last? How often will I wear it? What will it cost to maintain it, in cleaning bills and so on? This all boils down to the crucial question – what is the cost per wearing? If the answer to that is more than 5 per cent of your weekly income for one outfit, don't buy it.

As to the general style of what to wear, remember that you have more leeway in such industries as publishing and advertising than you do in conservative areas like banking and insurance. If in doubt, look at the men around you. If they are all in dark suits, you should stick to long-sleeved dresses and skirt suits in sober colours – black, grey, dark blue or green, maroon, brown or tan. If the men wear jackets and contrasting trousers, you can be a bit more casual and maybe even think of trousers yourself. What you must never do is wear a trouser suit which apes a man's business suit. It does not make you look like a businessman, it makes you look rather silly and attention-seeking. If you compound the error by wearing a man's tie with it, some of the men you meet will assume you are a lesbian and you'll have all that hassle to cope with.

Unless they are part of a suit, skirts are not such a good idea as a dress, especially if you have to keep tucking your top in. You shouldn't fuss at your clothes in the office, nor should your clothes fuss at you, so anything that makes a noise – which includes clanking bangles as well as skirts that rustle or swish – are out, because they have sexy connotations.

What you are looking for is a style that gives you authority, and this is best achieved by going for a tailored, even slightly military, look. Clothes that fit badly do not give you authority, so you will need to find somebody to make alterations for you. Work out the best hem length for you and stick to it, rather than play the fashion game of yoyo hems.

Shirts are better than blouses, unless you need a bow at the neck to soften your face. Even so, a beautifully arranged scarf does that job just as well. The main advantage of shirts is that you can buy men's shirts, even silk ones, for much less than the price of a woman's shirt-style blouse. If you have a big bust, buy a big shirt and get your tame tailor to make the necessary tucks.

Whether or not you have a big bust, never, never, *never* go to work without a bra. Jiggly breasts and protuberant nipples embarrass most men, and even if you don't believe that, remember it's your brain you're trying to promote, not your boobs. Dress like a sex object and you'll be treated like one.

Another thing that is classed as sexy is long hair, so either keep yours above shoulder length, or pin it up out of the way. Pinning it up may help to give you authority, as long as you do not allow tendrils to escape and then fiddle with them.

Something else that may help to give you authority is spectacles. If you want to get some, but don't actually need them – and I do know people who have done this to great effect – do get a pair with plain glass in, rather than no glass. Quite apart from the fact that the lack of glass is obvious in certain lights, you are bound to give the game away by poking a finger in the wrong place! Glasses really can be useful as a prop – you can look reprovingly over them at miscreants, take them off and wave them about to gain time when asked a tricky question and, best of all, 'forget' to take them into a meeting where some man may try to force you into the secretarial role of taking notes.

All your accessories should be carefully thought out with the same 'authority, not sex object' theme. Your shoes should be leather, fairly plain, low or medium height and always highly polished. (Powerful people always have beautiful shoes.) Your jewellery, if you wear it, should be genuine and tastefully understated and it should not get in your way. If you have an engagement ring, this may sparkle – but nothing else should. Think along the lines of gold, silver and pearls, and you won't go far wrong.

Keep your make-up simple, too. Office lighting is seldom flattering, so you may want to wear some, but avoid elaborate paint jobs round the eyes and leave your false eyelashes at home. Don't arrive in the morning with a bare face and retire to the ladies to paint it, but do make any repairs in private rather than at your desk. Incidentally, don't spoil the ship for a ha'porth of tar. Cheap make-up is obviously just that and so is cheap perfume. Better to wear none at all than to smell like a back-street brothel.

Forget all that nonsense about handbags that match your shoes, or accept it as another rag-trade ploy to part you from your money. What you need is a neat clutch bag and a beautiful businesslike briefcase to put it in. A briefcase automatically marks you as a serious executive. A handbag marks you as a 'little woman with her handbag to rummage in'. Haven't you noticed that men carry as little as possible? It's a throwback to the days when women carried a bag for the seeds and nuts they foraged, while the men carried nothing but their weapons to the hunt.

Be careful what you carry in your briefcase, in case

anyone sees inside. Avoid the secretarial trappings of notebooks and pencils. Better to go for a small battery-operated
casette recorder instead, then add a calculator and the
Financial Times.

If you must write on something, a pad of lined A4 is
preferable to a shorthand-type notebook, but do
strenuously avoid being inveigled into taking notes at meetings, *unless everybody else does so as well*. It is almost more
important at meetings to observe the body language of the
other participants than to listen to the words. You will be
able to work out their 'political' affiliations by watching for
signs of tension in the shoulders or anxiety in facial expres-
sions – and that particular information is always valuable.
If the meeting is one where you really must take in what is
said, then you should train your memory, even if it is only
for long enough to get back to your office and make notes.

This business about avoiding the secretarial tag really is
important. I do not mean to belittle secretaries *per se*, but
you must accept that being a secretary, no matter how
skilled, rarely leads to being managing director, any more
than being a superb nurse leads to being a brain surgeon.

In the eyes of the senior managers who are in a position to
hand out promotions, secretaries are people who operate in
a support role, not a managerial role, and if you behave in a
way that lumps you in their minds with the secretaries, that
is where you will stay. So – pretend you can't type, avoid all
the trappings (notebooks, arms full of files and so on) and
avoid the behaviour patterns. Don't gossip in the loo or
anywhere else, don't do your shopping at lunchtime (when
you should be getting to know your peers), don't do your
nails or eat at your desk – and *keep your private life to
yourself*. By all means let it be known you are interested in
music, or tennis, or that you have a lot of boyfriends, but for
heaven's sake don't give them blow-by-blow accounts of

each date. Don't witter on about your children or your husband's operation – and don't talk about your weight or being on a diet. If you need to lose weight, do it, but keep your mouth shut about it. (Come to think of it, keeping your mouth shut is the best way to lose weight.) It denigrates you to be forever on some new diet. All it does is prove you have no willpower and no control over your fate – not exactly the successful image you want to project.

And it is up to you to project it. If *you* don't do some personal PR, no one else will do it for you. It is an interesting fact that most people will accept your assessment of yourself if you give it to them. Unless they are rude enough to say 'liar' to your face, or sneaky enough to say 'true, true' to your face and 'liar' behind your back, the mere fact that they do not contradict you when you make your statement conditions them to accept it – and pass it on to others as their own opinion. Those others will in their turn pass it on whenever your name is mentioned, and it won't be long before your statement of 'I'm the greatest!' becomes part of office folk-lore. Equally, never miss an opportunity to let everyone know if you manage to achieve something brilliant. Use such successes to ask for new projects, a better job, more money or, at the very least, a bonus.

One of the best ways to acquire visibility, and many other benefits, is to find a patron or mentor. Don't confuse the concept of a mentor with that of a role model. A role model, in our business concept, is a woman who has achieved a high position, thus proving to you that it can be done. She need not even be aware of your existence. All that matters is that she exists for you to emulate.

Mentors can be of either sex, but must of necessity be higher up the ladder to help you climb. Their function is almost like that of a gardener who cultivates you and helps your growth. Boys are taught that they need a coach to guide their training and they carry this concept into their business life. They usually choose someone about ten years older than themselves (much more of an age gap and there is a danger that the relationship could become an over-close parental one).

A mentor is someone who can give perspective to your situation by letting you know how others see you, while at the same time speaking well of you in high places. He can give you valuable political advice, tell you who is dangerous and how to circumvent their venom. He can give you advance warning of disasters, or of projects you should apply for, with guidance on the approach needed to secure them.

In return, he will expect your support in his pet projects, and your loyalty. You must never abuse the confidentiality of his information and you must take his advice when it is offered – or at the very least explain why you prefer not to do so. He will see you as a protégé whose success will reflect on his astuteness in selecting you for his attention, and he won't bother with you for long if you do not prove to be worthy of his support.

You cannot expect him to defend you publicly when you have incurred your boss's wrath by some foolish error, but he can warn you in advance of how your various ideas will be received. For this reason he needs to have been with the company for some time, for his knowledge of previous successes and failures will be invaluable. He will be able to warn you of your boss's pet aversions and weaknesses, and will know of his soft spots and favourite projects. Being in a position to advise you in your relationships with your boss is possibly his greatest value.

One of the classic traps waiting for women arises from the fact that your boss may appear to need managing.

Maybe he does, or maybe he just likes to have you hand him everything on a plate, but the danger arises when your habit of managing him leads you to ignore or dispute his instructions. His priorities may not match yours, or his pet project may seem to be totally pointless – but *he is in charge* and that means you have to accept and carry out his orders or suffer the consequences.

Don't argue about it when he tells you off about this or any other mistake. Accept the blame, whether it was your fault or his lousy instructions (and there's a lesson for you – next time make *sure* you know what he wants!), and take immediate action to rectify the error.

You will be amazed at how quickly you'll be forgiven and back in his good books. If you want to stay there, ask yourself what he wants of you and take steps to provide it. It is a typically female attitude to say, 'Here I am, this is me. If you don't like the way I am, hard luck!' This attitude is irritating at the best of times. It is especially so to a person who feels his superior position entitles him to cooperation, not a blank wall. Irritate him enough and he will take steps to remove the irritant – and it will not be in an upwards direction.

Another major irritant for your boss is the subordinate who continually presents complex problems, with no proposals on how to deal with them. If he has to deal with the whole thing, he may wonder why you are there at all. Not only does he not want to have to do your job, he doesn't actually want to know all the details of how it is done, either. All he wants are the essentials to help build up his broad picture.

You are there to save him the time and effort of getting the details himself. He wants you to tell him what you've done, not ask him what to do. He wants suggested solutions and reports of action and progress – and he wants them in a form he can easily assimilate.

People vary tremendously in the way they accept and process information. If you can work out their favoured method and aim your delivery appropriately, it will be more meaningful to the recipient. The simplest version of this concept is that people are either readers or listeners.

A reader wants to be presented with words on paper that he can look at. A listener cannot cope with that and wants to be told. Readers are also writers and are happiest dealing with people by letter or memo. If you stand in front of one and try to tell him anything in detail he will ask you to let him have a report. When he talks to people on the telephone, he ends up by saying, 'Put it on paper.'

The listener is happier with a telephone in his hand than a letter and if you present him with a report he'll glance at it, put it down and ask, 'What does it say?' When you have to put anything on paper for him, keep it brief or preface it with a short summary. Incidentally, do be sure your definition of the words is the same as his. 'Cat' means tiger as well as *Felis domesticus*, and to a civil engineer it means a large piece of tracked machinery for earth-moving. 'Report' can mean a four-colour glossy brochure, a typed document or a person standing in front of a desk saying, 'This is what happened.'

The very least you should do is consider whether you are dealing with a reader or a listener. There is much more, however, and it is worth considering it if you want to get the best results from your communications. Let us go back to our furry friend. 'Cat' is a word on a piece of paper or a small animal which moves in certain ways and does certain things with its tail. It is also a series of noises – yowl, mew or purr. It also causes painful scratches, a warm heavy feeling on your lap and pleasant sensations when you run your hand over its fur. To most of us, one or other of those impressions of the animal predominates.

This is because we favour one of our senses above the others. People are either thinkers, lookers, listeners or feelers. Present them with a piece of information and they will deal with it in their favoured way.

Thinkers will apply logic to it, work out all the permutations and come up with considered answers. They choose their words carefully, for they want to be precise. They respond well if you use words like 'logically' and 'precisely' or ask them 'What do you think?' and 'What is your opinion?'

Visualisers compare everything with the pictures in their memories and tend to gaze at the ceiling or into the middle distance while they search their visual records. They will get irritated if you interfere with this process by standing at their point of focus and will feel uncomfortable if your clothes clash with their office colour scheme. They respond well to 'I see', 'Show me', or 'How does it look to you?'

Hearers hold silent dialogues with themselves and may get so involved with the discussion that they never get around to making a decision. They have expensive sound systems in their homes and cars, turn to music for inspiration or comfort, and their speech patterns are chosen to sound good as well as convey information. They like to be asked 'Can I talk to you about it?' 'How does that sound?' or 'Does that ring any bells?'

Feelers (I hesitate to use the word 'sensualists' for that is a little heavy in this context) are interested in sensations. They surround themselves with items that are nice to touch and frequently handle their clothes, person and the things around them. They tend to move around a lot – not nervous-fidgeting, but slow body movements because they like the feel of it. If you don't care to be handled, keep your distance.

Tell them you 'feel lukewarm' about a project, want to 'get a grip' on problems, or 'are in touch' with the people with the answers.

Before you dismiss all this as 'salesman's tricks', let me point out that sales people are taught these techniques because they are a proven way to gain rapport with prospective customers. You, too, are involved in a selling situation – selling yourself to people who can influence your career.

Here are a few more guidelines to achieving rapport. People are at their most comfortable when they are with other people who breathe at the same rate, and feel vaguely uncomfortable when other people do not, although they are unlikely to know why. Take the trouble to study your boss's breathing rate and try to match yours to it. Then you can alter yours and he will subconsciously match you. Since slow breathing means calmness and fast breathing means excitement, you can de-fuse an upset boss by bringing his breathing rate down in this fashion, or get him to find some enthusiasm for your pet project by speeding it up. To break the spell, just take a deep breath and move away.

You can match your voice speed and rhythms to his as well. Why do you suppose Americans from the Southern States hate Northerners so much? It's because the damn Yankees talk so fast – and the Northerners think the Johnny Rebs are stupid because they talk so slow.

The final thing that every salesperson knows, whether selling life assurance in suburbia or carpets in the souk, is that you must watch the eyes. Thinkers shut them, visualisers look up or ahead, listeners look sideways (presumably because that is where their ears are) and feelers look down. And people who are interested in something have an involuntary reflex which dilates the pupils and raises the eyebrows. This widens the eyes fully so they can see better.

Men do it when they see a pin-up picture. Women do it when they see a man they fancy – and men do it when they see a woman with her eyes dilated. It is one of the oldest known sexual attractants (hence 'Belladonna' – the plant that supplied the drops Italian ladies used in their eyes to make their pupils dilate).

The Chinese do it when they see a piece of jade they covet – and your boss will do it when you come up with something he likes. Keep your eyes on his eyes and you'll know when you are on to a winner. Pupil-dilation cannot be controlled, only hidden by dark glasses or disguised as a response to light conditions. It is another reason why you should keep your back to the window and look into a dark office.

As well as being a most important part of your feedback system on the people you are dealing with, it is your final weapon in the fight to get people interested in you and your work. Suss out their favoured acceptance distance, match their breathing, subtly raise it to excitement level, look into their eyes – and widen your own. Practise in front of a mirror until you have sufficient control to do it delicately so no one notices it is deliberate. Then apply it at work and see how it improves your relationships with subordinates, superiors and peers.

Your relationships with those outside your chain of command are every bit as important as those within it. Your boss may think you are marvellous, but if every one else despises you, you won't get very far. No department can operate in a vacuum, and good relationships make everybody's life easier.

Which is where the dreaded office politics raises its ugly head. It really is nothing to be afraid of as long as you don't let yourself get involved in inter-faction fights. It is only natural that people will congregate in groups of like-minded people who will then seek to support each other. The problems arise when two factions are both striving to gain prime position.

You would be wise to remain on friendly terms with all by refusing to take sides. That way, no one can regard you as an enemy or deliberately set you up as a scapegoat. You could end up with no friends if the only ones you have are the fair-weather sort who see you as no more than an aid to their ambitions.

Beware of voicing your scorn for the incompetent who continues to hold a responsible job when he patently does nothing but waste time and money. There may be a good reason for keeping him that you don't know about. (I met one of these some years ago and fortunately was told he was the Founder's illegitimate son before I made a fool of myself.) Don't make suicidal intolerant noises until you have all the facts. Even then, learn to accept the male sports-field mentality which says there has to be a full team to play at all. It doesn't matter if one of the team has to be carried, as long as they let you play in it.

Find out who are the real influencers of opinion. They are not necessarily the obvious ones with titles of power – what matters is that they have the ear of those who do. That insignificant clerk may be the daughter of the chairman's wife's hairdresser. Someone else may be related to a major shareholder or an important customer. And don't ever underestimate the managing director's secretary.

Then there are the support workers – the people in the post-room, the photocopier operators and telephonists – whose ill-will can make your life very difficult, or whose good-will can grease the wheels of day-to-day life. These are the only people with whom you should even begin to gossip. They tend, from the nature of their jobs, to get the news first, but they are always very grateful for additional snippets and never disclose their sources. I have always found them to be very nice people, too.

The wise gossip listens a lot, says 'ooh' and 'aah' in the right places – and contributes nothing but the totally trivial. Or the occasional deliberately calculated leak.

Other than that, the main piece of advice has to be to work out the corporate culture and conform to it. Don't insist on doing your own thing or you will stick out like a sore thumb. That is not the kind of visibility you need. Don't wear your pink boiler-suit to work in the bank. Don't park your Porsche in the company car park if everyone else at your level has a small Ford. And don't use bad language if the board are all devout church-goers. That will get you noticed, but not the way you want, and not the way that will advance your career.

4 Some problems men don't have

One of the arguments used to rationalise the male reluctance to allow women into the upper echelons of any organisation is that we are unable to handle stress. What they actually mean is that we do not handle it in what they consider to be the correct way, which is to pretend it does not exist. You are supposed to bottle it up, keep a stiff upper lip and generally present the world with the impression that you are perfectly in control of the situation.

What you are not meant to do is display any form of emotion. It is considered to be vulgar and embarrassing, not the done thing. And yet this 'correct' behaviour is one of the major contributing factors to the shorter male life-span.

It is accepted by the medical profession nowadays that bottling up your emotions is one of the routes to a heart attack, stroke or ulcers. The fact that women indulge in tears at stressful moments is one of the reasons we have fewer of these illnesses than men.

Constant pressure to perform and to succeed; frustration at blockages; the need to avoid time-wasting, deal with other people and still present the 'acceptable' image of a businessman; and the overwhelming fear of failure are the reasons men adopt what are known as 'type A coronary-prone' behaviour patterns. Until recently, few women have been in this position and consequently women have only represented a very small proportion of the sufferers of stress-related diseases. Even now that there are more of us working in the stressful high-level occupations, we still have our safety valve of tears to fall back on.

But although we are able to reduce the health-damaging results of the stresses that men suffer, we have a whole series of other pressures to deal with that are unique to our gender. The major pressure is the chauvinistic aggression shown to us in the office merely because we are women and fail to conform to the comfortable, unthreatening stereotypes some men prefer. This is such a large issue on its own that I have devoted the whole of the last chapter to dealing with it.

Many of us suffer from isolation when we are the only woman operating above the supervisor level in our company. It is easy in such a situation to imagine we are there as the 'token' woman used to demonstrate compliance with the Equal Opportunities legislation. Added to our other problems we then have the dread of being 'found out' as so incompetent they won't even want us as a token. If you are guilty of such thoughts, abandon them immediately, for they are nonsense. There are too many competent people on the employment market today for any employer to waste money on the other sort. Yes, I know I mentioned the 'gotta have a full team' syndrome earlier – but that only applies to men, I promise you.

If you are really feeling isolated, go hook yourself into a network, even if you have to get on a long-distance train to attend meetings. There are plenty of other women in the same situation and plenty who will serve you as role models, if that is what you lack.

The real difference between men and women is that a man is considered a success if he is good at his job, and a woman is not considered a success unless she has all the feminine virtues as well. You could be chairwoman of ICI, but two-thirds of your acquaintances would still judge you on the cleanliness of your house.

I don't want to get side-tracked on to the feminist platform, but we seem to have allowed the world to persuade us that nothing short of perfection is good enough. You can be a businesswoman if you want, but you must also be the perfect wife, mother, lover, hostess and housekeeper.

This gives you three options – do it all and run yourself into an early grave in the process; neglect some elements and feel guilty about them; or decide to do the things *you* want and to hell with the rest.

The first is a non-starter as a lifetime plan. I don't think too much of the second, either. If you live on your own, you can solve the whole thing by taking all your clothes to the dry-cleaners, entertaining in restaurants and adopting a 'your place, not mine' rule with lovers. If you don't live on your own, what are the others doing while you rush round doing your 'perfection' act?

We have a perfect working arrangement in our household. He has a job which frequently keeps him out late in the evenings. I have a full-time job, spend two nights a week at college and a lot of my other time researching and writing books. I do half the housework, half the cooking and put things in the washing machine but I DO NOT IRON SHIRTS. I don't wear them, so I don't care if they are crisp, so he has to iron them himself. He *hates* it, which just proves my point. (Dear Reader, please tell all your friends to buy a copy of this book so we can afford to pay someone to iron his shirts and make him really happy.)

Joking apart, what I have is a man who accepts that my commitments are as important to me as his are to him. If your co-habitee doesn't have this acceptance, it may be because you haven't taken the trouble to explain the matter to him. Or it may be because he rates his life and concerns as being more important than yours. In which case, either shut up and get on with your housework – or ask yourself the question 'Do I *really* need him?'

This question is the key to the stress thing. Come to think of it, it is the key to the whole business of getting control of your life. I assume, since you have read this far, that you have already decided you need a management career. If you are finding it difficult to reconcile that need with the rest of your life, you are going to have to examine each part of it and decide which bits you need most.

Which brings me back to where I started. If, when things get tough, you want to shout and scream or burst into tears, you need to make a rapid decision on whether the tension-releasing value of 'being emotional' is what you need right then. Or would you rather avoid embarrassing the men around you, retain your reputation as a cool lady, and hang on to it until you can be private?

On the whole, you will find that icy politeness and a steely expression is more likely to gain you the upper hand than an outburst of temper. The trouble with getting noisily angry is that many of us get so mad we burst into tears and ruin the effect.

If you do feel the tears coming, it is best to make the most dignified withdrawal you can – a touch of temper, as in 'How dare you!' is useful – and retire to the ladies to recover. Take deep breaths, drink cold water, splash it on your face and bathe your eyes. If there are teabags available, dunk them in cold water and hold them against your eyes to prevent inflammation. You will, of course, have to make a detour on the way to the ladies to collect your make-up kit.

If it is anger, not tears, do the deep breathing and cold water drinking, then go back to your desk and find something redundant to destroy. If there is nothing handy, take the paper out of your wastebin and tear it into little pieces. Bad language helps, too, but you need to check who is within hearing range before you scandalise them.

The trouble with all this is that you tend to end up annoyed with yourself for having succumbed to your emotions. By male rules, having to go away to calm down means you have lost the battle. If you find it happening too often, run through some practice situations in your head. Rehearse what might be said, and how you would feel and react, until your reactions are cooler. Then think of some appropriate cutting remarks and you are all ready for the next encounter.

Incidentally, do you have horrid dreams of being chased or attacked by monsters? It is not unusual, most highly-motivated women do – psychologists say it stems from their high valuation of themselves – and it is often triggered by stressful incidents at work. There is no need to worry about it unduly, unpleasant though it is at the time. But a wise woman does not put 'nasties' into her sub-conscious by watching horror films or reading horror stories. That is not the best way to relax, and relax you must if you are not to crack under the strain. The trite suggestion is to 'leave your work at the office', but that is not easy. It is impossible if you are studying as well.

The answer is to divide your life into compartments – work, study, housework, husband, play, and relaxation. Then avoid letting one activity run over into a compartment allotted to another. The only exception to this is that there are many domestic tasks which do not require your brain. Ironing, hoovering, washing-up, all these are times when you should be thinking ahead and planning the rest of your week.

What far too many of us do is fill our heads with noise during these 'mechanical' tasks, either by watching television or by listening to the radio. Do you really need to know what is happening in Ambridge or Dallas? Do you really need to spend an hour listening to someone pontificating on what *might* happen if this or that candidate wins a by-election?

I went the whole hog and refused to have a television at all. That was three years ago when my beloved and I set up home together. Neither of us misses it at all. If there is anything we particularly want to see, we watch it at my mother's. I'm not suggesting you get rid of your set, but I do suggest you apply the 'do I need to?' question to every programme. Get a video and tape the stuff you really want to see and watch it when *you* want to, not when it is transmitted. That way you will not be trapped into watching the next programme when the one you wanted is over.

Another major time-waster at home is unexpected visitors. The ones you have invited are no problem, for you are expecting them, but no matter how sociable you are, the ones that just drop in unannounced are a nuisance. They are intruding on your privacy and you need to get that message across to them. If it means saying 'I'm just going out' and getting in your car and driving off every time they turn up out of the blue, then do it until they understand the way to get your time is by pre-arrangement.

None of my friends would dream of doing it and neither would I intrude on them this way. Mind you, I've never quite had the nerve to copy one lady I heard of, who had a sign by her doorbell that said 'This bell has been disconnected. If you are expected, knock. If not, don't bother – I won't answer.'

What do you do about the non-friend interrupters? I have evolved a simple technique that works with all of them, from brush salesmen to Jehovah's Witnesses. (Honest!) It is this. Open the door, stare at them, wait long enough to be sure it isn't the man from the football pools with a cheque, say 'Push (or something else) off, I'm busy,' and shut the door. They go away. They don't come back.

It is only by rigidly excluding such time-wasters that you will be able to get some time to yourself for conscious relaxation. If you have children, you may have to lock yourself in the bathroom for half an hour to soak in delicious scented hot water. Even without the children, a hot bath is always a good way to unwind. Alternatively, lie down in a dimly lit room. Breathe deeply and slowly and empty your mind of all its cares. If any stressful thoughts intrude, visualise them written down on a piece of paper and mentally tear up the paper and throw it away.

Another technique is to tense your whole body, then relax it, joint by joint, starting at your toes and working up. Take a deep breath at each joint relaxation.

Breathing is an essential part of all relaxation techniques. There are many routines, but I find this one works for me. Breathing both in and out through the nose, pull in your stomach, flatten your diaphragm and raise your ribcage as you breathe in, then reverse the procedure as you breathe out. The whole thing is like a wave advancing and receding. As you breathe, you count, and the four actions of breathing in, holding the breath in, breathing out and holding the breath out, must all take the same length of time. As you practise you will be able to lengthen the times and this is part of the object of the exercise. Your count of 1,2,3,4, will extend to 5,10,15,20. Don't be in any hurry over this, it could take weeks to get that far. It doesn't matter if you don't. What matters is the rhythm. You will eventually find that as your breath control increases you are actually able to slow your heartbeat.

If you are unable to relax on your own, join a class in yoga, transcendental meditation or whatever is available locally. You will find they all rely heavily on breathing exercises and you must keep looking until you find one that suits you. Don't write them off as 'cranky' – they work. But you have to give them a good length of time. There is no such thing as instant relaxation and it may be some months before you begin to reap the benefits.

You really ought to make the conscious effort to relax for a minimum half hour every day, but if that fails make sure you have at least one unstressful day at the weekend. We stay in bed most of the day on Sundays. Toast, coffee, newspapers, nattering and snoozing takes us halfway through the afternoon, then it's up to the stables for a ride, back home for dinner, then, as often as not, back to bed by eight with a good book and a bottle of wine. You won't be able to do that if you have children. Then you should try to devote the day to them, or the garden, or those videos, or anything – as long as it isn't connected with work.

Don't tell yourself you haven't got time to relax. If you don't do it voluntarily, you might have it forced on you by illness. You can't afford to be ill, not if you want to get up that ladder. Nor should you let yourself be unduly inconvenienced by menstruation – which does not mean that I intend to class it as an illness, although half the men of the world seem to regard it in the same light as they would some awful contagious disease.

Many societies and some religions look on a menstruating woman as something impure and prohibit contact with her. It goes back to the days when no one knew it had any connection with getting babies. If men bled, it was because they were hurt, and they often died as a result. Women bled every month and they didn't die – so it must be witchcraft!

We know better, but we, as a society, still make a great fuss about it. Some single women make all sorts of excuses not to go on dates rather than admit they have a period. Some married women even try to hide it from their husbands, which is absurd, for even the dimmest husband must be aware of the mood changes that occur during the monthly cycle.

There's the problem – the mood changes. Most of us react to some extent as the end of the month approaches. Some of us get very tense and tetchy. We are hell to live with and hell to work with, and anyone with the ability to count to twenty-eight can work out why. The snag is that some men interpret any difficult moods as PMT and follow the old taboos of impurity by being rude and scornful.

If you do not care for your workmates to know your monthly cycle, you will have to take steps to prevent the outward signs. You should try to organise your work schedule to keep stressful activities away from difficult days. You could take a couple of days off each month, but this will soon erode your holidays. You could try the vitamin B routine. It works for some women. Or you could go to your doctor or a family planning clinic and ask to go on the Pill.

This might be considered a rather extreme course. Obviously if you do go that route you must consider your age, your blood pressure and so on, and then you may have to try several different types of pill before you find one that doesn't give you boils or morning sickness. You may well be throwing up your hands in horror at the idea of feeding your body a regular dose of drugs and artificial substances, but you should consider this. You are not meant to have a period every month – you are meant to be pregnant, permanently. It is the natural condition for the female, from menarche to menopause. We are baby machines and our bodies do not respond well to a monthly 'bounce' of hormones up and down as we ovulate and menstruate.

And what does the Pill do? It tells your body you are pregnant and lets you get on with your job without two-weekly mood changes. When you stop taking it for a few days, it produces a predictable (like down to the hour) period, with little hassle, little pain – and no PMT. There is one other advantage. It gives you the option of deciding exactly when to have your period. If it isn't convenient you just keep taking the Pill for another couple of days to postpone it. You can do what a lot of people believe the high-fliers amongst us do naturally – have your periods at weekends.

Actually, what most of us do at weekends is our house-work. No matter what your standards, you are going to have to do some unless you can afford to pay to have it all done for you.

There are several companies around now who will move in with a team and do a complete spring-clean in one day, then come back fortnightly or monthly to 'top up'. They do it all, from laundry to curtains, and they are not that costly, considering how much of your time they are saving. It depends on what you want done and how big the place is, of course, but I'm told that the spring-clean for a two-bed-roomed flat would be around £250 and the top up about £50. The alternative is a 'daily' who comes in on a regular basis. Some are more obliging than others, but you establish what they will and should do when you take them on. This method has the advantage of providing someone in the house to deal with the meter man or washing-machine repairs.

If you can't afford to pay someone, or don't want anyone in your house when you are not there, you will have to do it yourselves. The first necessity is to decide what you feel should be done and what needn't. If you are hardly ever in the place and don't mind a messy environment there will be less to be done regularly than if you are always at home and need beautiful things around you.

Do remember that it is *you* who lives there, not your mother-in-law. If she really feels the place should be immaculate, maybe she would like to keep it that way herself. After all, why pay an outsider when you could keep it in the family?

My solution has been to ignore most of it except the kitchen. My prime requirements are to be warm and dry, have a hot bath every day, clean clothes and a hygienic environment in which to prepare food and eat it. I don't mind dust on the mantelpiece or cat hairs on the carpet. As I explained earlier, I do not like unexpected visitors, but I do like to entertain, so I combine all this in regular dinner parties preceded by a major clean-up. Your priorities will be different, but you must work them out.

The only fair arrangement is that, since all habitees contribute to dirtying the place, all should help to clean it. They should most emphatically look after their own personal space and items, unless a trade-off can be arranged. (I wash his underwear with mine, he cleans my shoes as well as his.)

Plan the environment itself to be trouble-free. Pale carpets need constant attention to stay pale. Ornaments need constant dusting. It is possible to live graciously without them. Dark-coloured baths are a menace, especially if you live in a hard water area. Beds with sheets and blankets take longer to make than beds with duvets, but tall beds with coverlets that hang down to the floor are a wonderful place to hide clutter in an emergency.

Learn to think like that when you are furnishing and you will make your life much easier. Learn to carry things in both hands when leaving a room and you will save two trips. Better still, and especially where food is concerned, get a trolley and do it all in one trip. If at all possible, have your washing-machine and tumble-drier in the bathroom, so dirty clothes can be taken off a body and put straight into the machine.

Spend money on good kitchen equipment. Non-stick saucepans, food processors, slow cookers and kettles that switch themselves off. Electric plugs with on/off timers built in. A big deep-freeze and a microwave oven. Then learn the cooking techniques to make the most of them. Don't just cook enough for one meal – make a batch and freeze some. Freeze stuff in plastic or waxed paper containers rather than foil, so the whole thing can go in the microwave. Don't shop more than once a week, less if you have a big enough freezer. Buy ready-prepared vegetables and meat so you just have to dump it all in the crock-pot and switch on before you leave in the morning. Think about it all and let your head relieve you of slaving over a hot stove at the end of a busy day.

Teach your children to cook as soon as they are able to do so safely. Boys as well as girls – you don't want to be responsible for lumbering some unfortunate girl with looking after your son all his life. Teach them to do other domestic chores too, and make sure they do their share. You do not do children any favours by letting them grow up without learning that they have to work for what they want.

Teach them to think for themselves. Don't tell them your decisions, consult them when there are decisions to be made. If they are part of the decision-making process, they will be proud to carry out their share of the work. They will also learn to accept as totally natural the fact that you have a responsible job and will even feel sorry for their friends whose mum stays home all day. Your sons will make excellent husbands for the next generation of working women and your daughters will start their careers with none of the in-built difficulties we have to counter.

You will have to give some careful thought to what older children are going to do in the period between school ending and you/your husband getting home. Precisely what this activity should be is something only you can work out, but it should be laid down as obligatory. Left to their own devices they can soon get bored, and boredom leads to mischief.

Younger children will have to be met from school and kept under someone's watchful eye until you arrive. I do not pretend this is going to be easy to organise, but that is one of the costs of being a working mother. You must have such things well organised, for you cannot leave work halfway through the afternoon because your child-minder has not turned up. Nor can you fail to go in because measles has struck.

You know jolly well that children do get the standard ailments, and it is up to you to ensure that your back-up system is sufficiently well organised to cope with it. What children want when they are ill is to have someone familiar within call. If it can't be Mummy, it must be someone else they know and trust – which is why you should take care to stay on good terms with mother-in-law. You may need to call on her for sickroom duty.

It is a big step to employ live-in help with your children and housework. Whilst the wages are not necessarily that expensive, you must provide decent accommodation and food. You also lose much of your privacy, since you cannot banish the poor woman to her room in the evenings. Nor can you expect her to do all the grotty jobs and leave the nice ones like baths and bed-time cuddles for you. If you expect her to be devoted to your children, she is entitled to her share of their affection and some job satisfaction. Proper nannies, incidentally, do not do general housework. They look after the children and their clothes, clean their room and cook for them, but no more. To cut the cost a bit, you may be able to share a nanny with a neighbour, or local friend.

Au pairs are another matter. Whether they are treasures or disasters is very much the luck of the draw. Some nationalities are more dependable than others, but even the good ones are only with you for a year.

Au pairs you organise through special agencies. Nannies and other live-in domestic help you find through the advertisements in *The Lady* magazine. If you are dubious about either, on the grounds that it will unsettle your children, don't be. If you inform them nonchalantly that someone is coming to live with you to help you to look after them, they will accept it as normal. Just be sure you comment, equally nonchalantly, that she doesn't have to stay if they hate her.

What is damaging to a young child is to leave it at a badly run day-nursery. Before you commit yourself, check the place out thoroughly. Be especially wary if they have frequent changes of staff. Young children can cope with a lot, if it is familiar, but they do find a series of strangers unsettling.

This is only part of the planning you must do well in advance when you make the decision to have children and carry on working. There has been much talk lately about the 'biological time-bomb' ticking away inside us, the one that urges us to procreate before it is too late. Do be sure that it is *you* who wants to breed, not some outside pressure like your mother or his. There is an implied criticism that you are not truly a woman if you have not borne children, and it can be so easy to succumb to the pressure.

There is no great hurry about it. You can now safely have your first child at forty, and at that age you should have got your career well established and yourself sufficiently together to cope with the logistics of it all. You will note that I am assuming that the decision and the timing are under your control.

It is your body and your life. If you don't want twenty years of hard labour bringing up a child, don't let anyone pressurise you into doing it. If you are sure you really want to do it, just try to pick a time when it will not damage your career.

With or without children, if you want a husband, you are going to need an emotionally secure man. The insecure sort can create an incredible amount of psychological flak. They feel threatened by your success or your higher salary. They are convinced you are up to mischief with all the men in the office. They feel you should devote all your attention to them and they can make life very difficult.

If you have one like this already, it's time for Macdonald's Question – 'Do I *really* need him?' If you are courting a man who won't let you pay for anything, who isn't interested in your job, who gets annoyed when work commitments prevent you falling in with his plans, beware. You could have hold of a died-in-the-wool CPP (Chauvinist Porcine Person – can't call them Male Chauvinist Pigs any more, it's sexist).

Thinking about all my married friends, many of whom run dual-career marriages, the combination that seems to work best is that of temperamental opposites. One tends to be phlegmatic, the other volatile and short-fused. The latter goes off like a bottle of pop after a good shaking, and the former administers a pat on the shoulder and says, 'There, there, darling, never mind. Calm down.' It tends, in my experience, to be the wife who fizzes, but it is not always that way.

Which one are you? And more to the point, where are you going to find the paragon you seek as your opposite?

It isn't too difficult to meet people when you are young – you can run with a pack of like-minded friends to discos, sports clubs and so on. The problem is what to do when you are over thirty and all your friends are married. I'm not going to go through all the hoary old women's magazine stuff about evening classes and so on. What you want is a successful man who will regard you as an equal rather than a threat.

So you need to work out where the lonely, successful men go in your part of the world. Lonely? That's right, men have all the problems we do over finding a partner. They want a mate just as much as we do – and I do mean a mate, not just a provider of sex.

Look for them at meetings of the Chamber of Commerce, the British Institute of Management or your professional association, conferences and trade fairs. Do not scorn the recreational sources either – the squash club, the flying club. Do you know what it costs to learn to fly? It is not a sport for the losers of this world.

Don't pretend to be someone you are not. Only CPPs want submissive fluffy little creatures and if you pretend to be one, a CPP is what you'll get. Successful, mature, well-balanced men find successful, competent women tremendously attractive.

Don't allow yourself to be so anxious to find yourself a man that you get into dangerous situations – don't go looking for Mr Goodbar. Don't fall prey to married hyenas on the prowl. The distinguishing marks of this brute are a reluctance to give you his phone number, evasions when you want to go to his place rather than yours and a tendency to recite the Three Great Lies. What are they? The first is, 'My wife doesn't understand me.' The second is, 'I'm getting a divorce.' The third is not suitable for publication! Quite frankly, you would be better advised to buy yourself a dirty book and a vibrator than to end up despising yourself for waking up with yet another inconsiderate louse in your bed.

But don't give up. Quite apart from the obvious benefits of a stable relationship, it takes much of the heat out of your relationships with the men at work. You no longer need to view them as possible mates, and they no longer have to suffer the anxieties of either having to repulse you or, worse, taking you to bed and having to put up a satisfactory performance.

Please, please, do everything you can to avoid having an affair with a man at work, particularly a married man. I know you will forget all this if the chemistry is right, in which case all I can say is 'be discreet', but it will probably be the death knell of your career prospects in that company.

What it does is to put you immediately into that sex object role you have been trying to avoid. You may never have been to bed with another man in your whole life, but it will be assumed that you are easy. Your dignity will be permanently damaged and your judgement will be questioned. Don't think you can keep it a secret. It always gets out and, once one person knows, they will all know within ten minutes.

If it ends, you and he are going to have a difficult and embarrassing relationship to deal with. The only way out is for one of you to leave. Guess who it will be, and compute the odds of it being a career-enhancing move.

5 Managing your time

Whatever level of your career you are at, one area which needs careful thought is that of time management. It is not an exclusively female trait to be terribly busy all day with no real achievement at the end, but it is an easy trap to fall into, especially if you have come up through the ranks and been used to having a million things to do.

Taking work home on a regular basis is little more than an admission of inability to perform your job in the allotted time and it must eventually sap your performance through lack of relaxation time. Staying late in the office is actually worse, because the word will soon get around if you make a habit of it and then everyone will know you can't cope. Don't kid yourself that they'll see it as conscientiousness, or that they'll think well of you if they do interpret it this way. Secretaries are conscientious – managers manage!

There is an old saying that goes, 'When you are up to your neck in alligators, it is difficult to remember that your prime objective is to drain the swamp.' But a good drainage scheme is the only answer to the problem and the sooner you recognise it and take steps to organise one the better.

So how do you go about it? You need to do an exercise split into three main areas: what you do with your time now; what you ought to be doing with your time to be more effective; and what, to carry on with the analogy above, I'll call 'alligator' recognition and avoidance – for alligator read time-waster.

There are many individuals and organisations who make a living out of time-management courses and seminars. They all go about it in slightly different ways, but they all agree that you need to assess your personal goals before you do any detailed planning on an hour-to-hour basis. You'll flounder around in your swamp for ever if you don't know which bit of dry land you're heading for.

First task, then, is to find out exactly how you spend your time now. It won't be easy, but try to list, day by day, for the last week and the next one coming, just what you did with each half hour, both at work and in your leisure time. Be honest – there's no point in fooling yourself. If you were wasting time, list it. Next, make a list of all those activities, in order of the amount of time you spent on them, and then put that list aside. Then, on a clean sheet of paper, take a few minutes to write down all the activities you feel you ought to be doing (whether or not you are) and reorganise this list in order of importance. Now compare this list of desirables with the list of actuals and the odds are you will get a nasty surprise at how much time you are spending on low-importance activities.

At this point, you need to back off from the whole situation and ask yourself a couple of fundamental questions. 'What do *I really* want to do with my life? What do I want to achieve?' List all the answers, however silly they may seem. No one is going to see this except you. Want to be managing director? Stinking rotten rich? Famous? An Olympic gold medallist? Retire early and write romantic novels? Bum around the South Pacific on a tramp steamer? The possibilities are endless.

Set yourself a time limit and, when you've reached it, look over what you've listed and once again rearrange the list in order of importance. Then ask yourself the less open-ended question, 'What do I want to achieve in the next three years?' If you really want to do any of the items on the lifetime list, you'll find the same themes occurring in this one, with a touch more realism.

The final list may seem a bit off-key, but it is relevant. If you knew you only had six months to live, how would you spend them? It must be pretty obvious that no one is going to list work projects and, since this is a book on working, you may be wondering about the relevance. It is this: if you totally sublimate your personal life to your job you are likely to lose perspective and waste your time on unimportant matters. That way lies failure.

A well-balanced, successful person is usually one who understands the importance of relaxation. Why not reward yourself by doing some of those things that are so important to you that you would devote your last few months of life to them? The logical conclusion to listing these things has to be to ask yourself the final question, 'If I want to do it that much, why don't I do it now anyway?' There are only three possible answers to that. Your relationship with another person or people will prevent you, or you cannot afford to do it, or you don't have time to do it.

I can't help you with the first. It involves personal decisions that must be yours alone. The second should solve itself as your career progression brings increased financial rewards. The third can be cured if you are prepared to invest a little of the time you think you haven't got in reorganising yourself to use your time in the best possible way – which is the reason for all this list-making. Once you understand what it is you want to achieve, you can produce some realistic plans to lead you to achievement. If you don't know where you are going, you cannot even begin to plan the route and you can waste a lot of valuable time going up blind alleys.

Go back to your first list, the one of all the things you did last week, and see if you can use it to map out the coming week. Are there any daily tasks there which could be dealt with on a block basis, like letter-writing? Think about it – if you spend an hour each day answering letters, and each day's letter-writing session involves fifteen minutes waiting for your secretary to collect her book and pencils and come into your office, you would save a good hour a week by having a weekly session.

Are there any tasks which you do that could be done by someone whose time costs the organisation less than yours? The classic example of this is opening and sorting mail, which offers splendid opportunities for distraction and is a total waste of your time. I've often suspected it is done in fear of something incriminating arriving in the post, because there is no other reason for stopping your secretary doing it.

Another classic time-waster is that of reading the newspapers every day – 'in case there is something relevant to my job'. No doubt you should read relevant items, but the whole newspaper? More sense to avoid the possibility of getting side-tracked by letting your secretary or a junior go through the paper and mark or highlight the bits you ought to see. And if you want to see items on a private hobby list as well as work matters, all that is needed is a different coloured pen.

Your own reading time would be better spent on technical books or trade magazines. If you are daunted by the sheer amount of print involved, you may be tempted to learn speed-reading. The principle behind it is that you should take in blocks of print, rather than read each word individually. This means you don't move your eyes across the page but straight down the middle. Your peripheral vision should take in everything up to the margins, instead of being wasted on blank paper as it is when you scan back and forth.

Train yourself with the aid of a timer. See how much you can read in ten minutes, then each day try to take in more in that time. It doesn't count if you don't take in what you have read, but you will find that your eye will latch on to significant words and alert you to the need for a little more attention to that passage. I am not entirely convinced that speed-reading is the answer, as no matter how fast you read, you still end up taking in more information than you need.

It is better to read selectively, and this is easily done. Almost all non-fiction books have a table of contents at the front and an index at the back. These will give you a rough idea of the content of the book. Then all you need to do is glance at the sections that should interest you and read them carefully if they actually do apply to your situation. Make notes on a file card, not only of the title and author, but also of pages that you find particularly useful, and it is then easy to find and reread those pages later.

Are there any tasks you do that *should* be done by someone else? By this I mean the ones that you were suckered into doing by someone who took advantage of your innocence. If so, and that someone is not your superior, take the trouble to write a memo saying, 'Sorry, this is outside my frame of reference and I can no longer spare the time for it' – and make sure your boss gets a copy.

Are there any regular tasks you do that don't really need doing at all? Just because your predecessor did them or you've always done them doesn't necessarily mean they should still be done. Take the time to ask the recipients of the end product how valuable they find it and you could well find they never look at it, only use a small part of it, or only need it once a month instead of every week.

How much time do you spend writing letters that say, 'I haven't got around to doing it yet, but I hope to soon'? And why don't you spend that time doing the job instead of apologising for not having done it? How many letters do you dictate all the way through when they could have been dealt with either by use of standard paragraphs on a word-processor, or that your secretary could have written herself in response to your comment, 'Tell the old fool to drop dead!'

Once you've weeded out all the things you don't need to do, you can concentrate on the jobs you should do and start thinking about priorities. If you have difficulty with this, remember that anything related to the past is history. Unless it is an official return or an urgent need to cover your tracks, it should have low priority. Items that will make a real difference to the future should always take precedence.

Get a fresh piece of paper, list all the jobs you have to do. Decide which are the really important ones and mark them A or TODAY. The not-quite-so-desperate ones you mark B or TOMORROW, the next batch C or THIS WEEK and the rest Z or SOME TIME. The final job is to define the A list a little more by marking each task A1, A2, A3 etc in order of priority. There is no need to do this with the Bs or Cs, as they either become As or go away. Zs almost invariably do go away – and here is one of the values of this system, in that by labelling a job as being of small importance you don't waste your time in doing it.

If, instead of listing all your tasks, you prefer to organise them into piles, you can do so, or even jot each job down on a 3" by 5" file card. To a certain extent you can leave your secretary to juggle the piles into their current priority. The important thing is to list each task as it comes to mind, because you can then forget it. No point in cluttering up your head with 'things to do' when you can let a piece of paper do it for you.

The simplest method of doing all this is to keep a notebook for the purpose. Carry it with you at all times so it is handy for jotting things down when you think of them, then consult it every time you pause and wonder what to do next. As each job is completed, cross it off and move on to the next highest priority. Resist the urge to do Cs because they are easy and can soon be crossed off your list.

Whenever it gets untidy or difficult to read, just rewrite it. Do this at least once a day anyway, to refresh your mind and check your priorities. A good time to do this is first thing in the morning, when you have seen what is in your post and know if there is anything new that needs to be dealt with urgently. When you are fresh in the morning you are more likely to tackle a major task easily and less likely to be sidetracked. You will also have a new perspective on the tasks left over from yesterday and your subconscious may well have come up with the answer to one of yesterday's problems while you were asleep.

This often happens spontaneously, but you can take advantage of it by actually setting your brain a problem to deal with while you are asleep. The best method is a fairly casual 'now what should I do about so-and-so?' rather than detailed concentration, which is more likely to confuse the issue and keep you awake. Once you get into the habit of this you will find it frequently works and often produces a new angle that hadn't occurred to you before. But do take the precaution of keeping a notebook by your bed in case the answer comes at 3 am and is gone again in the morning.

If you find this does work for you, you may prefer to make planning tomorrow's work your last job of the day, as part of your wind-down before going home. If overnight answers don't alter the plan, you can start work on your designated first task first thing in the morning before the contents of the post arrive to distract you.

The same principles apply to weekly planning. You may prefer to start your week by planning it on Monday morning, or to wind down for the weekend by doing it on Friday afternoon. Whichever you prefer, you should try to produce an outline plan at least a week in advance, especially if you have a major task to tackle.

If you mark all the allocated blocks of time on a prominently displayed wall-chart, it will be quite obvious to visitors when you will have time for them. It is, incidentally, considered a sign of importance to have a full calendar, so you can also use this method to show everyone how much in demand you are.

Don't forget to take your monthly cycle into consideration and plan around it. If you suffer from two days of premenstrual short-temper, allocate those days to undemanding routine tasks and do the difficult or stressful jobs when you are in a better state to cope with them. If you don't already know it, find out your daily cycle too, and allocate alert times to difficult jobs and dull times to coffee breaks. (If dull times don't respond to short breaks and changes of activity, ask yourself if your eating habits are meeting your body's blood sugar needs or if you are getting enough sleep.)

All of which is fine as long as you have control of your own time. Unfortunately, a large part of any manager's time is commanded by other people and it is not always easy to sort out priorities. One key factor here has to be the status of the person asking you to do something. Another is the possible result of your failing to do it, or refusing. Clearly no one wilfully offends superiors in this way, but you could also be storing up trouble by ignoring requests for guidance from inferiors or requests for assistance from peers who may be politically inclined.

On the whole, and providing your refusal is polite, it is far better to say 'No' than to accept and fail to deliver, or take on too much and do an inadequate job of everything. Superb results from a few projects will get you a reputation for good performance far more quickly than trying to please everyone.

There is a theory called the Pareto Principle (after a nineteenth-century Italian economist) which says that 80 per cent of the results produced come from 20 per cent of the effort expended. This applies in all fields – 80 per cent of sales come from 20 per cent of customers (or 20 per cent of the sales force), 80 per cent of nuisance comes from 20 per cent of the people involved (and this is rarely the 20 per cent who are producing the results!).

Not only should you keep this in mind when setting your priorities, you should also consider it when allocating time for a project if you have a tendency for perfectionism. While in theory a virtue, do be sure before indulging it that you are not spending 80 per cent of your time in adding only 20 per cent of value to your projects.

Once you have set your priorities, all that is needed is to be left alone in peace to get on with the job. Which means eliminating those time-wasting alligators I mentioned before. The worst have to be the people who expect to have your immediate attention to their problem. It is irritating when your superiors do this and unless you have a *very* tactful secretary, difficult to overcome.

Where others are concerned all that is needed is polite firmness, both from you and your secretary. The first thing to do is to divide your time into blocks and decide which blocks are for you alone and which for contact with others. The next is to let the structure of your block system be known to all and refuse to see or talk to anyone during your private times unless it is a real emergency.

Get your secretary or the switchboard to intercept all your calls during quiet times and ask people to leave a number for you to call them back. Let it be known that an open door is an invitation for visitors and that a closed door may be opened by no one except yourself or your secretary.

If an open-plan office prevents this, learn to answer the question 'Have you got a minute?' with 'Not now – come back in twenty minutes.'

Don't give uninvited callers a chance to sit down. Either do away with a visitors' chair altogether or keep it piled high with more files than anyone would dare to move without being told. If the opportunity is there, get up to greet people at the door and remain standing, which prevents them sitting down and makes them go away sooner. If all else fails, take off your watch, put it on the desk face up and make it obvious you are looking at it and getting impatient.

If visits with subordinates are unavoidable, try to go to them rather than have them come to you, unless, of course, your business with them is of a private nature. This helps to preserve the idea that your own office is a private place, and has the added advantage that you can pick your own time to leave.

Tactfully let it be known that you prefer working to attending meetings and make a point of asking if your personal presence is essential when you are invited. If it is, press firmly for details of the purpose of the meeting on the grounds that you want to be adequately prepared. Ask how long it is intended to last and, if you dare, depart after the allocated time is up, having first taken the precaution of arranging another appointment.

If you have to hold meetings yourself, send out a detailed agenda with start and finish times. Let it be known that a summary will be sent out after the meeting inviting comments from those who did not wish to attend and make it clear that attendance is only required from people who have an active contribution to make.

Start on time and let late-comers catch up as best they can. Privately allocate a time for each topic and move the meeting on when that time is up. Don't let people wander from the subject and don't let them get too comfortable, even if that means cutting a chunk off the front legs of all the chairs. Finally, do everyone a favour by finding out how long their attention span is and curtailing the meeting before the cut-off point is reached.

One of the worst time-wasters at meetings is the bit at the end when you all try to match time in your diaries for the next one. This can be avoided by using a variation of the method used to check football pools coupons. Before the meeting, issue everyone with a transparency marked off in days and hours. Everyone puts a cross in the places when they are already busy and hands it in when they arrive at the meeting. Then all you have to do is put them together and hold them up to the light to see when everyone is free.

Or are you an alligator yourself? Quite apart from doing unnecessary jobs through the inability to say 'No', many of the major time-wasters are self-generated. Procrastination is probably the worst, especially where big jobs are concerned. The more important and complex the job, the greater the fear of failure. So instead of spending several chunks of time telling yourself 'I'll start it tomorrow', why not split it up into a series of little jobs which could at least be started in the same chunks of time? Don't allow yourself to rationalise putting off starting by thinking you'll be fresher tomorrow, or have a big block of time free, or just spend the rest of today clearing your desk so you'll have no distractions tomorrow. If you find yourself thinking along these lines, just stop it and tell the truth – 'I'm wasting time.'

Anyway, why put yourself through the agony of thinking about this horrid job and not getting any of the benefits of getting it done? That way lie ulcers and other stress-related diseases. We all know that dreaded jobs are never as bad as we thought when we get around to them, so why make such a fuss? Or do you get a kick out of narrowly beating deadlines? Fine – but what are you going to do when flu strikes the day before the deadline and you haven't even started? I know the answer to that so I'll tell you – waste even more time regretting your failure!

Inability to make decisions is not only a waste of your time while you vacillate, it is also an infuriating waste of time for the others involved. Like any other activity, decision-making becomes easier with practice. Write down the problem and list the alternatives. If there is no obvious best solution, ask yourself 'What's the worst that could happen if I'm wrong?' about each alternative and choose the one with the least frightful consequences. Then debrief yourself when you have seen the results and consider why you were right or why you were wrong. Remember, there are only two choices where decisions are concerned – the right one or the wrong one. If you are right more than half the time, your performance is above the statistical norm.

Another major time-waster is a lack of organisation. If you know where things are you will not waste either your time or your secretary's in searching for them. Mother's rule – 'don't put it down, put it away!' – applies in the office just as much as it does at home. It also deprives sanctimonious colleagues of the satisfaction of quoting 'an untidy desk is a sign of an untidy mind', although they may well be right. I have heard it suggested that an untidy environment leads to tiredness, on the basis that you actually expend energy by being irritated by the mess. In the long run, the cost of filing equipment will be less than the cost of your time.

Perhaps one ought to say, 'Don't put it down, *deal with it* and put it away.' The only pieces of paper that should go into a 'Pending' tray are the ones where you are waiting for a response from someone before you can complete the job. Everything else should be dealt with, passed on or binned. We call it 'round filing' in my office. I have heard it referred to as 'the noble art of wastebasketry'.

If you cannot deal with something on the spot, don't allow yourself to handle it more than twice – once when you get it and once when you deal with it. When it arrives, put it on the 'telephone' pile, the 'dictate' pile, the 'vital technical reading' pile, or the 'B' pile.

Better still, let your secretary do it. Encourage her to be more than a shorthand typist/filing clerk. Tell her what is going on. Give her daily progress reports. Let her deal with routine mail and telephone calls. Let her organise your priority piles and make sure she is at the top of your 'I'll always see/talk to' list. She needs three of these lists – 'when they want to', 'when I want to' and 'not at all'.

You'll get a lot of phone calls from people outside the company who want to sell something. Whether or not your area is the one that deals with such things, once the word gets around that there is a female manager, the sharks will gather in the hope of an easy kill.

Travel agents, conference organisers, training schools, office equipment or communications experts (the current one is car telephones) – whatever it is, it's big business. They will use all sorts of ruses to get past your secretary, the classic one being to use Christian names so she assumes it is a personal friend. She should have a blanket instruction not to accept Christian names without surnames and that if the name is not on the list, no dice.

And she never, ever, under any circumstances, gives anyone your home telephone number. I do a lot of litigation work and I was not amused when the defendant in one of my cases rang me at home. He should have been dealing with our solicitors, but he thought he could bully me into dropping the case and had told one of the girls in the office he was a personal friend.

If you are not in the office and someone insists it is a matter of life and death, your secretary rings you herself and tells you the problem. You can then get her to deal with it or ring the caller yourself. But if it's a stranger and they won't give a reason for needing to talk to you – sorry, no dice.

If sales people do get through to you, there is only one thing to say. 'Send me some details. I'll look at them and pass them on. Don't call us, we'll call you. Thank you. Goodbye!' With people you do want to talk to, you can save a lot of time by brushing up your own telephone technique, especially when you instigate the call. The basic rules are to keep it short and keep to the point. Both are easier to achieve if you have any papers you might need in front of you and make notes of what you need to say. It also means you don't forget anything crucial.

It is polite to ensure that you have picked a convenient moment to call, and to tell the callee immediately what you want. If you say something like, 'Hello Henry, Janet here. I need to talk to you about the new contracts. Have you got a minute?' it gives them the choice of talking now or ringing back, and no one is offended. If you make a habit of doing this, eventually people will get the message and do the same thing when they call you.

I log all my calls and make notes on what is said. I often find telephone conversations are disputed and it stops all arguments if you are able to say, 'We spoke about that at 3 pm on the 17th. You said thus and so. Would you like a copy of my notes?' If it is likely to be critical, I have my notes typed and put on the relevant file and I still have all my notebooks from when I started this job. You may not have that sort of job, but since you need to make notes on what you want to say and record the answers somewhere, why not do it in a bound notebook?

A lot of management books will tell you that you should not indulge in social chit-chat on the telephone. I do not agree. Obviously you should not waste your time and the company's money on prolonged nattering, but the social amenities help the wheels of commerce go round. It's always been said that 'it's not what you know, it's who you know', and this applies to women as well as the old boys' network. You can't know someone unless you talk to them as a human being rather than a work machine. And the higher you go up the ladder, the more you find is done on a social level.

There is also some dispute as to whether you should dial your own calls or get your secretary to do it for you. The do-it-yourself school says it takes as long to tell her as it does to dial, but that does not allow for engaged lines, a wait while the callee finishes another call, or wrong numbers. It is much easier to call back or call much used numbers with modern computerised telephones, but it still does not compare with a secretary working her way through a list of people you need to talk to. While you talk, she gets on with something else. While she dials, you do something else – like maybe dictating the tape for her to type from tomorrow.

This is another disputable area – do you use a dictating machine or shorthand? With the machine, she can be doing something else while you dictate and you can post tapes to her when you are away. If you are in your office, you can dictate the difficult stuff and give her the standard stuff to deal with herself. Shorthand is better for confidential matters and for building the relationship with your secretary.

One thing that is a must for any humane boss, is to get your secretary a proper dedicated word-processor. (Not a mini-computer with a word-processing program. I've used both and I don't care what the computer buffs say – word-processor is best.) If you produce any sort of complex material, or documents that run through several drafts, or just a series of standard letters, it will save an incredible amount of time and hassle – and it guarantees you perfect copy.

One final point about your secretary. She is in a position to add to and gather from the company grapevine. Don't give her any opportunities to put your weaknesses into it. Do use her to get what you need from it. Look after her to the best of your ability – she can prevent you putting your feet in a lot of wrong places.

6 Handling your staff

One of the primary functions of a manager is to get results from her staff. With our woman-skills of sensitivity and concern, it is a function that we should find easier to handle than men do, yet it is an area many of us shy away from.

I cannot imagine why. Without going very far back into history, there are plenty of precedents. The housekeeper with her army of servants, the matron with her nurses, the chairwoman and her committee, the typing pool supervisor, the teacher, the mother with her group of children – all of them capable of getting things done and many of them handling a series of complex and varied tasks leading to the desired end product. It is not even as though they were not controlling men, for many of them were.

Nevertheless, many women today do find this difficult, but we must grasp the nettle and learn to manage a mixed bag of staff or we will not rise above being supervisor of a small group of junior females.

The most important thing to remember is that your job is not a popularity contest. You are not there to be liked, you are there to get things done. You need to be respected. If you are also liked, then that is a bonus.

To be respected, you must be firm but fair. It is unfair to be seen to have favourites and for this reason it is not wise to socialise with individual members of your staff. Even joining them in a pub at lunch time on a regular basis makes it difficult to keep a distance between you. This doesn't mean you can never do it, just don't make a habit of it. Indeed, there are some occasions when you must join in – birthdays, wetting the baby's head and so on – but even then you will have to be careful what you drink.

You must make it clear that your instructions have to be carried out, but if the orders you give are likely to be unpopular it is only fair to give some explanation of their necessity, even if it is only 'the chairman wants us to do it', delivered with a wry smile.

To be respected, you must be seen to be as good at your job as your staff are at theirs. This does not mean you have to be better at their jobs than they are, but it does mean you have to know what they do in enough detail to be sure they are doing it properly. They know damn well if they are sloppy, and they also know you are meant to prevent it. They will not think you nice and easy to get on with, they will think you are a fool – a 'soft touch' – and they will take advantage of you.

They will also have a fair idea of the parts of your job that do not directly concern them and whether or not you are any good at them. If you are not in command of your job, they will be well aware of it. They will scorn you for it and they will pass this scorn on to their peers in other departments. It will filter upwards until it reaches the ears of your own superiors. If you have to stay up half the night mugging up on something to keep ahead of your team, so be it. It is part of the price of seniority.

One thing you will have to work on, when you first acquire a team, is your leadership style. You have a choice of two basic styles – autocratic or democratic. These are known in management training circles as Theory X and Theory Y.

Theory X assumes that people don't want to work at all and must be made to. To get them to do anything, they must be ordered, threatened and closely controlled. They have no ambition, don't want responsibility and can only be reached by bribery through the wage packet. Theory Y assumes that working is as natural an activity as playing or resting, and that people naturally want to produce good results. They gain satisfaction from using their ingenuity in solving problems, and most of them seek responsibility for their own function. Many actively seek to accept responsibility for others as well.

You will probably have a strong inclination one way or the other already. So will your staff and so will the company. You may find it difficult to apply Theory Y in a Theory X company without getting leaned on from above for your laxity. Your staff will take some time to realise you are not just weak if their last boss was Theory X. Whether or not you can get a better team performance your way will depend on how many of them are really Theory Y people themselves.

You will certainly not get a good response from Theory Y people in a Theory Y company if you apply Theory X. Sooner or later they will all leave and you will have to replace them from outside because no one will want to transfer internally. Which will soon prove expensive in advertising, agency fees and Personnel's time. It will not be long before they realise they have a problem – and it is you.

Whether you take the autocratic route and tell your staff what to do, soften it by explaining why, or consult them before deciding, they must clearly understand that you have the final say. You have to establish this from the very beginning. No sliding quietly into your new role hoping you won't upset anyone. There is a very high chance that one of the group hoped to get your new job, and that is sufficient reason for that person (and perhaps others) to resent you.

Don't try to make friends until you have sussed out the situation. Give it plenty of time – the disappointed pro-motee may well have chosen to be on holiday when you arrive and will not be immediately apparent. Never mind the 'I'm Mrs Nice' approach. Get 'I'm in charge' established first, then soften up later if the situation allows it. Use the tone of your voice and your body language to help establish your authority. Stand up straight, look them in the eye and make firm statements. 'I want you to do this' or 'Will you please do that.'

Soon after you move in, make the opportunity to have a private talk with each member of staff. It is easier to establish your authority on a one-to-one basis and you can assess each person while you discuss their job. Ask if there is anything they need, or any improvement they want to make, and wait for the feed-back. Try to have a specific small task for each one to carry out in the next week and use the result to establish the standards you require.

Maintain a distance between yourself and your staff, particularly if they have never had a woman in charge of them before. You will not get their respect if you try to be 'one of the lads', and with men, or older women, there are other dangers.

'Respect and obey your elders' does not apply in a work situation. Your elders, however, may not be happy with that. Older men are most likely to resent being told what to do by 'a chit of a girl'. Older women may try to press a mother/daughter relationship on you. Both need treating with firm polite tact. With younger men you just need to be firm. Not maternal – whichever way you try to play that one, it won't be the way his own mother is and he'll resent it. With men of around your own age you need to be even more careful. Don't permit any physical contact or any hint of sexual badinage. That gives him the upper hand and everyone else will assume the worst. With younger females it is much easier. With the odd bloody-minded exception, they will be in some awe of you anyway, and regard you as a role model. All you have to do is assume they want to follow you up the ladder and treat them accordingly.

If you have real problems, you will have to consider giving them the sack. Your credibility will not survive if you do not and you owe it to the others to remove anyone who is not pulling their weight or is contaminating the work environment with uncooperative attitudes.

Firing people is absolute hell. It is a task that everybody hates, but sometimes it must be done. There is a set routine of warnings, both verbal and written, that has to be gone through to comply with the Employment Protection Act, but it all comes down to the final crunch. You have to get the person in front of you and tell them, 'You're fired.'

Make it easier for yourself by preparation. Psych yourself up by finding something personal you dislike – their clothes, habits, political opinions or something nasty they said to or about you. Don't mention any of it to them or they will drag you to an industrial tribunal. The purpose of the exercise is to harden yourself against them. All you need to say is something like, 'You have been warned already that your work is not up to the required standard and given a chance to improve it. You have not done so. I am not prepared to keep you on my staff any longer.'

When it is done you need say no more to the rest of the staff than, 'John will be leaving us at the end of the month/ will not be back.' They are unlikely to make any comment, since they will all have been aware of the build-up to it. But they will all pull their socks up in case they are the next one on your list.

It rarely comes to such a drastic situation, but there will be many occasions when you will have to issue a reprimand or criticise a piece of work. General whip-cracking is quite easy. If they are getting noisy or boisterous when there is nothing to do and you haven't got anything for them, you say something like 'Keep the noise level down please' or

'Calm down, you are supposed to be working', both of which imply that you don't really mind but don't want the rest of the company to know. If they have got work to do, 'Settle down now' is a useful phrase.

Criticism of an individual's work should always be done in private. It is the work you are criticising, not the person, and you must not damage their dignity. Adopt the approach that this is a valuable person who happens to have produced a poor piece of work, as in 'You've made rather a lot of mistakes this week', not 'Your work is deteriorating.'

Don't tear the whole thing apart, just point out the specific items that displease you and why. Don't get involved in explanations or excuses. All you are concerned with is the fact that the piece of work is sub-standard. Don't go on about it. Don't bring up any other old grievances. When you have said your piece about it, let that be the end of the matter. To avoid being totally negative, find something in their work you can praise so they can depart on a high note.

Do your praising in public. People like to feel they are valued. They like it even more if everyone knows it. Keep an eye open for specific things you can praise and say why you like them. When the whole team has done a good job, say so. Make them feel good as a team. Use the words, 'Well done, team. You did a good job on that.' Reward them, even if it is only with cream cakes at tea-time, or a flower and thank you card on each desk next morning.

If you don't tell people when you are pleased, they will not know what pleases you, nor how to please you. They can't know they've got it right if you don't say so, any more than they can know what you want if you don't tell them properly in the first place.

There are many work situations where a task has to be performed in a certain way, either because that is the way management likes it, or because it is the only way it can be done. These tasks tend to be the ones done at a low level, or those done for an official purpose, such as filling in the VAT return. Teaching such 'mechanical' tasks to one who has never encountered them is a comparatively simple matter. All that is needed is to explain the steps of the task and the fact that it must be done thus and so. If it is done like that, it is right and good. If not, it is wrong and bad. Simple.

The higher you get on the ladder, however, the more complex and open-ended the tasks become. As often as not they involve examining a situation, considering alternatives and recommending one of them for action. When setting a team this sort of job, the situation is less one of instructing than briefing.

For an adequate briefing, you need to have done quite a lot of preliminary groundwork yourself. You must obtain all the available information and find out what additional resources will be available if needed. If it is a major company project, you need to know what is to be done by other departments to avoid overlap. You need to know of any 'no-go' areas, you need to know the parameters and you need to know the priority rating and the deadline.

Then you can call your team together and present the project to them. When you have given them the facts, you can give them your rough plan of action and see if anyone has any improvements to offer. The larger the team, the more the likelihood of someone knowing something you don't. Allow them some time for discussion, but be sure it is relevant. Finally, you can split the project into its component parts to allocate to the most appropriate group members and give it a priority rating with the other work of the department.

In such a situation, the more information you can give your team, the better the end result will be. It is stupid not to tell them everything you know. It is equally stupid to forget to tell them when it is to be completed, who wants it and in what format.

Even then, you cannot just go away and wait for the results. Although you may not need to do anything specific on the project itself, you have to be there in a support role. Even a well-knit team used to working together needs encouragement from time to time. They may need more information, computer time, an extra typist, or a junior clerk to go out for sandwiches.

You cannot know what they need if you do not monitor their progress. I once worked in a team situation consisting of three teams of four, reporting to a manager whose office was on the other side of the building. He had to come through our office to get to his, but he never even said 'good morning'. We spent much of our time seething over the poor quality of the information we received from other departments to work on, but nothing was ever done about it. The team leaders would be summoned to his office occasionally, but the rest of us were only called in for a reprimand. It was not a happy office and I was neither the first nor the last to transfer into another department.

At the very least you should check on your staff twice a day. Then you will know if they have any specific work problems. Better still, you should spend long enough with them at the beginning of each day to see if anyone is feeling low. They may have had a rude letter from their bank manager, have a child in hospital or just had a bad night's sleep. Even without intruding into their private life you can give a boost to their day by greeting them brightly and spending a little time with them.

It does no harm to de-brief a team immediately after a major project. Then any problems will be fresh in their minds. But it should also be done at regular intervals to evaluate the way they operate. They may feel they need some training in a specialised area, or they may have found a hidden talent in one of the team members that they feel should be given prominence.

A good team as an entity will be greater than the sum of its component parts. Its members will be so used to working with each other that they will develop a communication system that will be practically telepathic. For this reason it is rash to disrupt it by gratuitously removing or adding people, but it is a good idea to rotate their jobs a little. If you do not want to bring new people into the team, the existing members will need to have an idea of each other's specialities to provide cover during holidays or sickness. There is also nothing like doing someone else's job to give a different perspective on your own – and nothing like a new brain to see ways a job can be improved.

While it is necessary that the members of a team work well together, it must also be remembered that these people are individuals. To get the best out of them you must get to know them, for if you do not know how they tick you cannot know how best to apply pressure or assistance when it is needed. One of the old 'necessary' feminine attributes was to be charming. The word conjures up the image of a delicate lady sipping tea in her drawing-room, and yet it is no more and no less than to be interested in people and to let them know it.

If you have a large staff you will need to cultivate a good memory, for at the very least you must remember where each person lives, the name of their spouse and their main hobby. If your memory is poor, keep a prompt sheet on each person and consult it before they come into your office. Make sure your secretary warns you of birthdays in time to buy a card. (Her birthday should be prominently in your diary!) Don't keep a stack of cards in your desk – someone is sure to find out and that negates the value of the whole thing.

These personal details are your key to the conversations which will unlock your staff's personalities. Some will be straight-talkers who mean what they say and do what they say. Others are devious, never give a straight answer and spend half their time trying to work out what you meant by what you said. Some think they can fast-talk their way out of trouble and some are so far away in their heads all the time they hardly talk at all. Some need only the outline of an idea and will be offended if you try to explain the details, while others need to have the whole thing explained laboriously several times and still go away muttering, 'I don't understand.' You will need to vary your delivery for each one.

Some are larks, best in the morning, and others are owls and barely function at all before tea-time. It's no good trying to explain a new concept to them first thing in the morning. Some are meticulously precise and others reckon that some mud will stick to the wall if you throw enough at it – the 'rifle' or 'shotgun' approaches. And a few – but only very few, thank heavens – are just so damned obnoxious to everyone they meet that you will wish their work was sloppy so you could get rid of them. Their work, of course, is perfection, and you can't do without them!

But they all have their strengths and weaknesses. It is your responsibility to develop the one and lessen the other. Most people can be encouraged to develop by the simple fact that someone believes they can do so. They need opportunities to show their potential and earn recognition for good work. Show them that you will applaud attempts at improvement, successful or not and you will remove their fear of failure and encourage them to try again until they do succeed.

One of the best ways to do this is to give them a task that they have to do all on their own – and to let them do it. You'll need to brief them thoroughly, but once the task is given, you must not see it again until it is completed. Refuse to have anything to do with outsiders who want to draw you in to it. Just explain politely that you asked Tony to deal with it and that he has full authority to do so.

Don't tell him how to do it, just what you want done. Let him work it out for himself. It's *his* job, remember. It doesn't matter if he does it differently to the way you would, as long as the result is right. And don't just hand over the boring jobs. People will not develop without challenges. You should look at every job that comes your way and ask yourself which of your staff can do it, not wonder when you are going to find the time to do it yourself.

Delegation of the things you don't *have* to do frees you for the things that do need your superior knowledge. It also frees you to move on up and helps you to assess which of your staff can step into your shoes. Even if you have not been around long enough to think of moving up, you must still keep some free time. If you are always busy you will never be available when people need you and they need to know that you will find time for their problems.

Quite apart from knowing you will be available as a general principle, your staff need to know when you will be there. I mentioned 'open door' times in the previous chapter, but you will need to give some thought to the general area of time-keeping.

The rigid rule of 'nine to five' is very much relaxed these days. With all the problems of rush-hour travelling, many companies run some sort of flexible working-hours scheme. The more enlightened ones run a formal scheme, with 'core' times laid down, individual clocks for each member of staff to switch on and off and the facility to take last month's overtime as days off this month.

The company I work for uses it and it works remarkably well. Everybody knows *exactly* where they stand and whether they need to do a bit of extra time to make up, or can go home early if they are over the top and their workload is light. The larks come in early and the owls come in late and everybody is happy.

There is a school of thought that says the boss should be in first and out last. This implies a basic distrust of your staff which does not encourage them to think for themselves. My personal feeling is that you should time your arrival after theirs. That way, they have a chance to have a cup of coffee and talk over last night's TV before they settle down to work without feeling guilty because 'she' can see they're not working. It also means they are all there when you arrive and you only have to say 'good morning' once!

If that late arrival is likely to mean difficult travelling, why not emulate one of our London managers? He drives in from the country very early when the roads are empty, and is in his office well before eight. He does an hour's work in blissful peace and quiet and then he goes out for breakfast. He comes back at half-past nine, by which time the post has arrived and everybody has settled down to work.

But even in the most flexible of situations, there will always be someone who abuses it. With flexitime it is easier to deal with, for if the offender's clock does not have the requisite number of hours on it as the end of the month approaches, he is just going to have to put some more time in until it does. If not, it's off to Personnel and the disciplinary procedures.

Without clocks, you or your secretary will have to keep a detailed log of comings and goings. The confrontation, when you are ready for it, must include recorded and accurate facts, for the standard first line of defence in such cases is denial. Without proof, you cannot continue your reprimand and reprimand you must, or be unfair to the rest of your staff. Once the facts have been accepted as accurate, the second line of defence is inevitably a variation of 'I can't help it.' Your response should be to utilise your standard criticism routine. 'Your general performance is good, but in this respect it is poor. Other people manage to get here on time. You must learn to do so as well. I cannot tolerate continued lateness.'

You should then put on your counselling hat and examine the circumstances that cause the bad time-keeping. Whether the problem is a child with a torn sports-shirt, a social life that involves late nights and inadequate sleep, or a metabolism that takes a long time to get going, it inevitably boils down to failure to recognise that it is possible to control your life instead of drifting with the tide.

Tempting though it may be to point out that the answer is to go to bed earlier and get up earlier, that is not enough. You need to provide help by discussing and drawing up a specific plan of action. If it works, apply praise. If it doesn't, it's back to the drawing board to revise the plan for another try before applying the big stick.

This will not be the only occasion when you have to adopt a counselling role. Some of your staff will bring you their personal problems as well as work ones. While you should not necessarily encourage this, you should not reject it. Just be very careful what advice you give. Remember you are only hearing one side of the story and you should not make value judgements without all the facts. Try not to get involved – that is not what you are there for. Indeed, you will rarely need to, as what is normally needed is a sympathetic but impartial ear. More often than not, if someone has to explain a personal problem lucidly to someone else, it is enough to straighten it out in their mind and show them what to do. So your role here is that of a sounding board – and a totally confidential one.

The only situation where you may need to take some action is when the problem involves another member of staff. You should be prepared for this by checking out procedures with Personnel. There will be a laid-down company policy on most matters and you need to know what it is.

The commonest problem of this sort is sexual harassment. I'll discuss how you cope with it when it is directed at you personally later, but the problem here is how to deal with a subordinate victim. You must give her your immediate attention. (It is not unreasonable to assume it is going to be a female. It hardly ever happens to men and they would probably prefer to talk to another man if it did.) She is going to be upset, so you must talk to her in private. Explain that you will be taking notes in case she wants to make a formal complaint later, but that whether or not she does so is her decision.

Listen to her story. Don't comment on it, or on her reaction to the attack. Remember that something you would take in your stride as an older or more experienced woman can be deeply upsetting to a young girl or one who has led a sheltered life. Remember also that it is probably not the first manifestation – people don't normally complain until they have decided they can't cope on their own.

Once you have heard her story, let her calm down a little and ask these questions: 'Who was it? Where? When? What did he say? What did he do? Did anyone else see/hear? Has he ever done it before? Do you know if he has ever done it to anyone else?' And finally: 'Do you want me to do something about it? Do you want to file a formal complaint?' The answer to the last will probably be 'I don't know, I hadn't thought about that', in which case you lock your notes away until she has decided.

Don't do your 'tigress defending her cubs' act. Don't jump on the harasser. Don't complain to his boss. If you are asked to take it further by the victim, make your report calmly and impartially to Personnel. If she doesn't want you to do anything formal about it, then don't, but do mention it in passing to the senior woman in Personnel next time you meet her. No names, just, 'One of my girls complained that she was sexually harassed in the Bought Ledger department last week.' If the harasser is a habitual offender, Personnel will know about it anyway, but they will be glad of more evidence.

It is a major modern hazard. The incidents we hear about are only the tip of the iceberg. It is not sexual attraction, it is an aggressive dominance ploy and it is intended to be offensive. It is very difficult, if not impossible, to explain to our male superiors how offensive we find it, and therefore difficult for them wholeheartedly to implement its eradication. Which means it is up to us to act when it is brought to our attention.

7 Chauvinism and other male attitudes

I don't know who coined the phrase 'the battle of the sexes'. Whoever it was, I wish they hadn't. It is too often the case that the designation of a situation, especially with such a warlike name, inflames it and encourages it to grow out of proportion. It started, I believe, in America, where life is generally more aggressive than on this side of the Atlantic, and it escalated into a full-scale war. Many clever journalists saw the opportunities to be exploited, and from that grew the militant feminist movement and much of our current troubles.

Have you had much to do with animals? I don't mean gerbils or the domestic rabbit, I mean real animals – horses, cattle, even dogs. If you have, you will be aware that they are fine if you handle them in ways that do not alarm them, but that if you are rash enough to back them into a corner they are liable to attack viciously to secure their escape. *Porcus chauvinisticus* is no exception to this situation – nor to the following.

A high proportion of my job involves removing the snouts of various importunate people from the company trough, and my experiences have led me to evolve a theory – there is nothing so aggrieved as someone who is being prevented from continuing to do what they know damn well they should not have been doing in the first place. They seem to consider that because they got away with it at all, they are entitled to continue.

By attacking men on the basis that they have been depriving us of our entitlements (i.e. what they see as *their* jobs) and that we want them – NOW – the feminist movement has put them on the defensive. And everyone knows that the best form of defence is attack.

Not every woman with career ambition wants to achieve it by doing down some man. Most men are secure enough in themselves and their ability to do their job properly to see no reason why a competent woman should not do an equivalent job. The trouble is that there has been enough propaganda from militant women to frighten less competent or less secure men very badly. They have responded by attacking and they are not too fussy about who they attack. If it wears a skirt it is the enemy.

The sad thing about Western society is that the constant pressure to succeed has created a lot of insecure people. The classic cop-out for women has always been that they can dump the responsibility of looking after themselves on someone else and stay at home with the telly and the kids. Men can't do that. They have to go out and fetch home the bacon and the insecure ones are always on the defensive.

Their defences take various forms, many of them aggressive, the rest involving jockeying for position in internecine power games. They use all these defences against men when they see them as a threat, but they do at least wait until the threat from another man has become specific. With a woman the threat is inherent in her mere existence.

Since the whole thing is illogical anyway, it is hardly surprising that many of them revert to the primitive dominance ploy of sexual harassment. A minor but relevant side-track here. Baboon troops display many of the behaviour patterns I mentioned earlier. They have a definite leader, whose wish is law and who backs it up with very nasty teeth if he has to. He has many wives, who fawn on him and groom him and who share his high status. There is a definite hierarchy amongst the adult males – and when they have cause to chastise a subordinate, they emphasise their superiority when he surrenders by mock intercourse. Whether the subordinate is male or female, the gesture of surrender is to bend over. The superior then mounts and gives a couple of token hip thrusts – a sort of 'I'm in charge and don't you forget it!'

This pattern of behaviour seems to be part of our simian ancestry. In the minds of many men, their ability to force sexual intercourse on women is the mainspring of their supposed entitlement to dominance over us. Brute force has become equated with power, and power and sex have become ineradicably intertwined. Which is what sexual harassment is all about. It means 'I'm stronger than you. I can force you to submit if I want to. I can use you. I am more powerful.'

It takes many forms, from innuendo to a pat on the backside, from blatant sexual suggestions (including four-letter words) to more lingering intimate touches. It will probably start tentatively and, if you don't react strongly to repulse it, future encounters will get worse. So you might just as well get on with repulsing it straight away and save yourself more trouble.

It is not a good idea to make a major fuss. They are usually sneaky enough to have done it in such a way that they will be able to use a defence that puts you in the wrong – 'What is the woman on about? I only said . . .'

Don't pretend you haven't noticed. He knows damn well you have and will consider he has scored. If you protest later, he'll say, 'You didn't mind last time.' Your best bet is to say, quietly, something like, 'Don't do that to me. I don't know what you intend, but in my book it is sexual harassment. If you do it again I will repeat that statement loudly enough for the whole floor to hear, and I will use your name.'

Ask around to see if he has done it to anyone else. He is unlikely to do it in front of witnesses, but if it gets bad enough for you to want to make a formal complaint you are more likely to be believed if you are not the only complainant. Write it down in the form I suggested earlier. If you do get to the stage of making a formal complaint, you will need to produce something more accurate than, 'He's done it before, lots of times.' Remember that your accusation could have a serious effect on his career, and Personnel will be reluctant to act on vagueness.

What if the offender is your boss? To be blunt, there is not a lot you can do about it except try never to be alone with him until you can get a different boss. Ask Personnel for a transfer and tell them why without making a formal complaint. If they can't help you, find another job as soon as you can.

You will note that I have not suggested you may be over-reacting to what was intended as a friendly gesture. I know many men will say things like, 'When are we going to have a dirty weekend together?' and I know when it is meant to be badinage and when it is not. So do you. Trust your instincts and you won't go far wrong.

Another male dominance trick is to raise the voice or say, 'Shut up and listen to me.' There is only one way to respond to aggression and that is by assertion. Stand your ground and let it be known you do not care for bad manners. Say, 'You don't have to shout at me, Mr Bloggs, I can hear you perfectly well,' or 'If you will let me finish what I was saying you will find it relevant.'

Some men will fire questions at you and demand that you answer. It is not so much that they want to know the answer as to prove that they can make you do what they want. Clearly, your response must depend on the situation and people involved, and you must not lie under any circumstances, but unless it is your superior asking a direct question like, 'Have you done that report yet?' there is no reason why you should be railroaded into answering.

'How many salesmen have we got?' asked by one of these men, calls for a comment like 'Don't you get a copy of the monthly manpower figures?' – rather than 'Three hundred and sixteen.' 'Where are those figures I asked for?' from the same person gets him 'I'll be putting them in the mail to you when I've had them checked' – not 'I'll bring them up now.' And 'Where did you get that information from?' gets 'From my usual sources,' or 'I'm not prepared to divulge that but I can assure you it is accurate' – instead of 'My flatmate works in their typing pool.'

What it boils down to is refusing to be pressurised just because the other party is a man. The more they try, the more you refuse to give way and continue to state your case. Constant repetitions of the facts or your considered opinion will wear even the most aggressive man down eventually. Don't be side-tracked, don't allow yourself to get angry. Just stick to your point and wear him down with sweet reason.

Stay ultra polite. If you make the mistake of descending from your pedestal, you will be promptly dragged right down into the gutter. Obscenity can occasionally be useful, but this sort of situation is not one of those occasions. Unless you were brought up in a barrack-room, you are unlikely to have the command of language or idiom needed to win a swearing match.

Much of this aggression is linked to territoriality. Animals and humans share the territorial imperative, no matter how loudly some humans may deny it. Ever seen a big dog back away from a little dog defending his garden? The big dog knows he is in the wrong and does not consider his size an advantage in this situation. And it is part of the folklore of the motor car that if you hope to escape with no more than a ticking-off from a traffic cop, you must get out of your car and go to him. Your car is your territory and if you stay in it he is the aggressor and he will give you a ticket for making him accept that role.

So if you do have to deal with an aggressive man, you will always do better to go to his office instead of meeting on ground where he feels he has to assert himself. But strangely, this is often the man who will try to keep you out of his own office; it is almost as though he feels your 'invasion' of his territory will succeed. Take advantage of this by playing along with it until you want something. Then march in and ask for it and he will probably be so anxious to get rid of you, he'll say yes straight away.

If anyone makes a habit of coming into your office to harass you, you can easily counter this as long as it is not your boss. All you have to do is reach for your dictating machine and switch it on. There is nothing quite so disconcerting as knowing you are being recorded.

Some men get completely hooked on power. It stems from feelings of inadequacy that can only be assuaged by being in total control of their surroundings. We should all be in control of ourselves, but we do not all need to have everyone jumping at our commands. These men are particularly concerned with maintaining and increasing their prestige. Many of them actively compete in sports where winning means individual recognition, rather than in team sports. They go for aggressive sports like squash or fencing and they display their trophies in their office as well as their home.

They surround themselves with the trappings of prestige – big powerful cars, ostentatious watches, original paintings, Savile Row suits and gold credit cards. They do not want to know about your ideas, all they want is for you to do as you are told. To be fair, they are the same way with men, but they will not tolerate any form of what they see as insubordination. They do not make good bosses.

Oddly enough, it rarely occurs to them to consider a woman as a rival. Since his womenfolk at home are chosen to be impressed by his status, this type of man assumes all women will think he is brilliant when he tells them of his plans to grab more power. So all you have to do is train your mouth to say 'Oh, how clever, do tell me more,' when your brain is saying 'Sucker!'

He has fallen into the stereotype trap. There are not many situations where stereotyping runs to our advantage but this is one of them. A man who wouldn't dream of even thinking about his plans in front of another man will readily explain them to a woman. They are so used to thinking of us in a support role that they assume it is personal support of themselves. It is curious that despite seeing us in a subordinate role they still actively seek our approval by telling us what a fine fellow they are.

There is one other way you can take advantage of this male inability to see you as a rival. The combination of that and the fact that most of them have been brought up to be polite to ladies leads them to let us go into rooms first. Which means we get first chance at the best seat – the one that gives us maximum visibility and frequently precedence, too, if it is close to the bossman. It takes a lot of nerve to ask a woman to move when she has settled.

Make the most of it. It is about the only time a group of men will defer to you, particularly if you are the only woman present. They may pretend to – the classic example of this is to apologise for swearing – but what they are actually doing is pointing out that you are different, an interloper. Don't expect any of them to side with you against the others, not even your boss.

Especially not your boss, since for him to do so means he is abdicating in your favour. And don't make the horrendous mistake I made recently of sitting myself at the end of his desk, thinking I was ranging myself on his side. It took me ages to work out why he was so aggressive and awkward to me at that meeting, but of course it was because I had usurped his authority by invading his territory.

There aren't enough of us in management for men to be used to dealing with us, and most of them still don't know how to. Even the non-aggressive ones haven't worked out our role yet and both they and we have a great deal of awkwardness to work through until we are on familiar ground. The best bet is to stick to the fact that you are both there to do a job and that getting it done is all that matters.

Any man who will not accept you on that basis has to realise that his refusal to do so is clear evidence that his priorities need rethinking. Don't tell him so in public or he will never forgive you. Just work on getting the right tone of puzzlement into your voice when you mention it to people who will relay the message higher up.

They can play this one against you, though, if you are rash enough to complain about discrimination. It will be claimed that you are more interested in making trouble than doing your job and you will not get up that ladder if you get the tag of 'trouble-maker'. Anyway, who do you complain to? Not Personnel – that is not what they see themselves as being there for, unless your complaint is one which comes under any of the Employment or Equal Opportunity Acts. Even then, it is more likely to damage your career than enhance it. Not your boss, if it is someone in another department, because he will not want to encroach on someone else's patch. Not the offender's boss, because he will consider *you* are encroaching on his patch and impertinent to boot. Not your boss's boss, if it is your boss, because he will see it as disloyal. He will also deal with it by asking your boss what is the matter with you, and can't he keep his staff under control?

Let's face it, if you've got problems with people at work, you are on your own. The way to deal with them is to work out first whether you are the problem yourself, then adapt your attitudes; or find a way of dealing with the situation that fits into the corporate rule structure.

Historically, the business world has always been a male world and it has always operated on male rules. As more of us get into powerful positions the situation will change, but it will not happen overnight. In the meantime, like it or not, if you want to succeed you will have to accept the situation as it is and learn to live with it.

Which is not to say you must totally ignore your feminine responses and force yourself into male behaviour patterns. If you can prove that your abilities are valuable, they will be accepted on that basis, as will the results of your feminine intuition if they turn out to be consistently right. If you are good at this, 'legitimise' it by using the male word 'hunch'.

There can be little doubt that women think in a different way from men. We've always known it, but it has been fashionable lately to put it down to upbringing rather than something inherent in our body chemistry. But recent research work on brain function is beginning to find that male and female brains do work differently.

The brain is divided into two halves, known as hemispheres. The left hemisphere operates the right half of the body and vice versa. Certain specific functions tend to be dealt with in one hemisphere only; for instance, creativity is thought to be dealt with in the right brain and analytical logic in the left brain. In fact, most of the skills men excel in, and which have to date been considered essential for successful business management, are dealt with in that left hemisphere. The skills that are traditionally female are controlled by the right hemisphere – and so is intuition.

What this means is that we are more in touch with our intuitive ability than men, not that they don't have it at all. But this is the reason that 'sleeping on it' so often produces the solution to problems. It isn't that we don't have all the needed information in our heads, it is that we are blocking our brain's ability to sort it out by our habits of conscious thought. The stars are there all the time – we just don't see them in the daytime because the sun is too bright.

Few of us are aware of seeing patterns, although our ability to recognise them is critical to our business success. I mentioned before that you cannot get the best out of people unless you know what makes them tick. The skill comes in being able to take a few pieces of observed behaviour and recognising them as belonging to a familiar pattern. It is a highly developed version of this ability that makes a chess Grand Master. They cannot compute the variables of each move, there are too many pieces on the board. It would take a computer *years* to do it, let alone a human.

It is the reason why a good salesman rarely makes a good sales team manager. All his brilliance is in recognising the patterns that tell him which way to pitch his approach to a customer. He may not be able to recognise patterns in his team's behaviour that he needs in order to get the best performance from them.

The more you observe and absorb the patterns around you in your work environment, the easier you will find it to make the decisions you need. Many of these patterns will be of chauvinistic behaviour. The sooner you accept that, the sooner you will be able to rise above it to the realms where your ability to do the job will bring you your just rewards.

It ain't easy – but then it ain't easy being a bored housewife either. If you can get up to the top of that ladder the view will far outweigh the effort of climbing. Just remember the words of Woody Allen – '80 per cent of success is showing up.'

Appendix **Networks**

You are not alone. There are many organisations which exist solely to help women, and others which now recognise the need to help women as part of their main function. Some provide training, some information; some actively lobby for women's career interests and others exist to provide networks.

For a complete list write for the booklet entitled 'Women's Organisations in Great Britain' to the
Women's National Commission,
Government Offices,
Great George Street,
London SW1
(telephone 01 233 4208).
Some which have come to my attention are:

The Adwomen
This is an association of women in advertising, marketing and publicity. It was formed in 1963 to help, support and advise the many young women entering the industry and continues today for support, contact, caring, learning – and fun.

They welcome prospective members at their regular informal evening meetings in London.
Details from: Sue Peters,
The Progress Agency,
2 Park West Place,
Kendall Street,
London W2 2QZ
(telephone 01 402 9361).

British Federation of University Women (BFUW)
This Federation is open to women with degrees from British or foreign universities (including Open University, CNAA etc) or approved equivalent

professional qualifications as Ordinary Members, or
students in the final year of degree courses as Junior
Members. Your subscription also makes you a member
of the International Federation of University Women, so
members form a chain of friendship and communication
internationally as well as nationally and locally.

There are local organisations which have regular
meetings with good speakers, and there are also regional
and national meetings. Nationally, BFUW corresponds
with and sends reports to MPs and ministers,
representing the views of women graduates; helps
women graduates serve the community in all areas of
public life; helps women in all countries towards better
opportunities for education, training and research; and
works for equality for women in many fields.

Details from: the Secretary,
Crosby Hall,
Cheyne Walk,
London SW3 5BA
(telephone 01 352 5354).

British Institute of Management (BIM)

The BIM runs a whole range of courses for managers,
and has recently added some intended both for women
themselves and for all managers who want their
organisation to benefit more from the creative ability of
women. Courses are open to non-members of the
Institute as well as members.

The BIM is currently actively seeking to recruit
women members at all levels. Membership is subject to
assessment, with the grade of membership depending on
academic qualifications and managerial experience. If
you are really serious about increasing the female 'voice'
in influential business areas, this is an organisation you
should make every effort to join. There are over a
hundred branches throughout the country which have
regular meetings.

Details of both membership and courses from:
BIM,
Management House,

Cottingham Road,
Corby,
Northants NN17 1TT
(telephone 0536 204222).

City Women's Network
The City Women's Network, starting from a predominantly
financial and legal membership base in 1978, is now
open to all senior professional women in London. It has
a monthly luncheon with a guest speaker and a range of
evening meetings, from the educational to the social.
    Details from: 58, Coleman Street,
London EC2R 5BE.

The Industrial Society
This is a very large independent organisation, which
aims to promote the fullest involvement of people in
their work in order to increase the effectiveness of
organisations and the satisfaction of individuals. It has
some 16,000 member organisations, ranging from
industrial and commercial companies through
nationalised industries, central and local government
departments and employers' associations to trade
unions.
    It specialises in leadership skills, communications
and consultation, productive management–union
relationships, conditions of employment and young
people at work. It provides training courses all over the
country on a wide range of topics – and more
importantly for our specific interest, it runs a special
unit for women's interests – the Pepperell Unit.
    The Pepperell Unit aims to help industry and
commerce maximise the talents and energy of working
women, and it was formed in response to organisations
concerned about the under-utilisation of their female
staff; government organisations such as the Manpower
Services Commission and the Equal Opportunities
Commission, anxious to promote and implement
equal opportunities; and individual women who are
interested in the opportunities and challenges offered

by industry and commerce.

Of particular interest are the courses run by the Pepperell Unit, many of these in conjunction with *Cosmopolitan* and *Good Housekeeping* magazines. There is a four-day residential 'Development Course for Women', aimed at those women who are seen by their companies as having management potential but who lack the self-confidence to push themselves forward; a 'Saturday Development Course' for women who know they want to give more and get more out of their work but lack a sense of direction; a one-day conference called 'Divided Loyalties' which seeks practical answers to the problems and stresses of balancing a career with bringing up a family; and others on Job Mobility, Coping with Pressure, Putting Yourself Across, Your Second Chance, Developing Your Woman Power, as well as career workshops.

They also do a very cheap two-hour 'taster' career workshop in the evenings – but all their workshops and courses are affordable and the accent is on participation and self-development. (Author's note – I have attended some of these myself and strongly recommend them.)

Details from: The Pepperell Unit,
The Industrial Society,
Robert Hyde House,
48 Bryanston Square,
London W1H 7LN
(telephone 01 262 2401).

International Toastmistress Club

This is an international organisation, but it has groups all over the UK, which meet twice a month. They have educational sessions in a supportive environment and provide opportunities to practise organisational leadership and speaking skills in situations that provide immediate feedback – a great confidence-booster.

Details from: Cecil Massey,
10 Cranberry Place,
Southampton SO2 0LG
(telephone 0703 227167).

Network
This was started in 1981 by a small group of senior
women working in London, who wanted to provide a
way women at their level could meet their peers, build
up contacts, share interests and discuss mutual
problems. It has now built up a thriving membership
representing a wide range of interests from the
professions, commerce, industry and the arts.

Amongst their mutual aims is the encouragement of
women to seek senior professional and managerial
positions. The basic qualification for membership is two
years of managerial, executive or senior professional
experience.

There are monthly meetings, workshops, discussion
groups and seminars, a Network Directory and a
quarterly newsletter. As well as London there are
currently branches in Edinburgh, Glasgow and
Manchester and links with groups in Holland and New
York.

Details from: Irene Harris,
25 Park Road,
London NW1 6XN
(telephone 01 402 1285).

**National Organisation for Women's Management
Education (NOWME)**
This was formed to respond to the need for a
coordinating organisation which could act as a focus
for information on development in management training
schemes and company policies aimed specifically at
women; and as a resource service to companies,
personnel managers, training officers, women managers
and other women wishing for a management career.
It also aims to act as a national network for its
members.

As well as evening meetings (held mostly in London),
workshops and courses, it offers a directory of members
by region and occupation, and a quarterly newsletter.

Details from: Lene Orchard,
29 Burkes Road,
Beaconsfield,
Bucks
(telephone 04946 2360).

UK Federation of Business and Professional Women
This is one of the largest organisations, with a
membership of around 10,000 women in nearly 400
clubs throughout the UK. Its main aim is to help women
achieve their full potential, and it constantly pressurises
the government for equality of opportunity in education,
training and employment. It strives to ensure that the
voice of moderate women is heard and that women are
in a position to influence decision-making at all levels.

It runs seminars at various locations throughout the
UK, and a series of workshops on the confidence-
building skills (Interpersonal Skills, Effective Use of
Time, Assertiveness, and Public Speaking). At the time of
writing these are held in London and Yorkshire, but
there are plans to take them to other areas and to widen
the range of topics.

It has recently embarked on a series of 'Young
Careerist' competitions, open to women up to the age of
35, designed to encourage the 'high fliers' of the future.

Details from: the General Secretary,
23 Ansdell Street,
London W8 5BN
(telephone 01 938 1729).

The 300 Group
This group was formed in 1980 to seek the equal
representation of women in Parliament and all political
forums, and to assist, encourage and train women to
seek and hold public office. It is non-party and works
across all party lines. It welcomes women who want to
help and support other women as well as those who
want to stand for office themselves.

The 300 Group offers training for public and political
life, holds fringe meetings at all the main party

conferences, and has many active regional groups.
Details from: 9 Poland Street,
London W1V 3DG
(telephone 01 734 3457).

Women in Banking (WIB)

This association was formed in 1980 to provide a
supportive organisation which would encourage women
to develop careers in the banking industry and promote
their professional image. Membership is open to all
women in the banking industry, regardless of whether they
are formally involved in lending money. Those who have
left the industry but intend to return are also eligible.

WIB meets monthly in London and provides seminars
and workshops as well as high-calibre speakers at its
meetings. Local groups are currently being set up
throughout the country.
Details from: Philippa Greaves,
c/o Saudi International Bank,
99 Bishopsgate,
London EC2M 3TB
(telephone 01 638 2323).

Women in Publishing (WiP)

This group was founded in 1979 to promote the status of
women in publishing by encouraging networking,
providing support and training, and campaigning within
the industry.

As well as having monthly meetings in London, WiP
organises regular training days, publishes a monthly
newsletter (*Wiplash*), holds an annual conference and
presents the Pandora Award each year for the most
positive contribution to the status of women.

Women in Publishing has members in many different
countries, and there are sister groups in Oxford and
Dublin. Membership is open to all women working in
publishing and related trades.
Details from: Gill Negus,
31 New Road,
Old Harlow, Essex.

The Women's Engineering Society
This worldwide society was incorporated in 1920 and
still promotes the study and practice of engineering
among women. They organise meetings of women
engineers and scientists, welcome student and junior
members and offer career advice and support to
individuals and schools.
  Details from: the Secretary,
  25 Foubert's Place,
  London W1V 2AC
  (telephone 01 437 5212).

Women in Management (WIM)
This group aims to promote better utilisation of the
nation's womanpower, to give women support with their
career ambitions and to encourage companies to make
better use of their women staff.
  There is a 'learning arm' of rising junior managers and
a solid core of established senior managers and highly
paid specialists. There is a good mix of business and
professional members, which gives excellent
opportunities for networking.
  It holds major events from time to time and presents
regular discussion evenings (held in London), executive
lunches for senior women, and it publishes three
newsletters a year. Members also receive *Women and
Training News*.
  Details from: 74 Cottenham Park Road,
  Wimbledon,
  London SW20 0TB
  (telephone 01 946 1238).
  WIM's founder, Eleanor Macdonald (no relation to the
author) also runs a training consultancy which holds
regular training courses on Personal Effectiveness,
Assertiveness, Team Building, and Career Development
both in the UK and overseas.
  Details from: 4 Mapledale Avenue,
  Croydon,
  Surrey CR0 5TA.

Women and Training Group
This group was set up in 1979, to promote women's
development through training. It organises conferences
and workshops, identifies approaches to meeting the
training and development needs of women, and
disseminates information on experience of successful
strategies, techniques and methods.

It publishes a quarterly newsletter, *Women and
Training News*, which includes details of recent
publications and forthcoming seminars, workshops and
courses. It is sponsored and supported by the Manpower
Services Commission.

Details from: Anne Cooke,
GLOSCAT,
Oxstalls Lane,
Gloucester GL2 9HW
(telephone 0452 426836).

Select Bibliography

These are some of the books which have helped
formulate my thinking, and some others which you may
find useful.

Ardrey, R., *African Genesis* (Collins, 1963)
——, *The Territorial Imperative* (Collins, 1967)
——, *Hunting Hypothesis* (Collins, 1976)
Barash, D., *Sociobiology – the Whisperings Within*
  (Fontana, 1981)
Berne, E., *Games People Play* (Grove Press, 1964)
——, *What Do You Say After You Say Hello?* (Corgi, 1975)
Bollies, R. N., *What Colour is your Parachute?* (Ten Speed
  Press, 1983)
Buzan, T., *Use Your Head* (BBC Publications, 1974)
——, *Use Both Sides of your Brain* (E. P. Dutton, 1976)
——, *Speed Reading* (David and Charles, 1977)
——, *Speed Memory* (David and Charles, 1977)
Conran, S., *Superwoman* (Sidgwick and Jackson, 1975)
Daily Telegraph, 'Women in Management' (Fact Sheets on
  Career Building)
Drucker, P. F., *The Effective Executive* (Pan, 1970) (and
  many others)
Durden-Smith, J. and de Simone, D., *Sex and the Brain*
  (Pan, 1983)
Eagle, R., *Taking the Strain* (BBC Publications, 1982)
Fensterheim and Dell, *Don't Say Yes When You Want To
  Say No* (Dell Books, 1975)
Friedan, B., *The Feminine Mystique* (Victor Gollancz,
  1963)
Golzen, G., *Changing Your Job* (Kogan Page, 1981)
Gurley Brown, H., *Having it All* (Sidgwick and Jackson,
  1982)
Harris, T. A., *I'm OK/You're OK* (Pan, 1970)
Heller, R., *The Naked Manager* (Barrie and Jenkins, 1972)

——, *Superman* (Magnum, 1979)

——, *The Once and Future Manager* (Associated Business Programmes, 1976)

Hennig, M. and Jardim, A., *The Managerial Woman* (Marion Boyars, 1978)

Jay, A., *Management and Machiavelli* (Dryden Press, 1967)

Korda, M., *Power in the Office* (Weidenfeld and Nicolson, 1975)

Lakein, A., *How to Get Control of Your Time and Your Life* (Peter H. Wyden, 1973)

Mackenzie, R. A., *The Time Trap* (McGraw Hill, 1975)

McClelland, D. C., *Power – the Inner Experience* (Irvington, 1975)

Miller, R. and Alston, A., *Equal Opportunities – a Careers Guide* (Penguin, 1984)

Morris, D., *The Human Zoo* (Jonathan Cape, 1969)

——, *The Naked Ape* (Mayflower, 1977)

——, *Manwatching* (Panther, 1978)

Page, M., *The Company Savage* (Coronet, 1974)

Peters, T. J. and Waterman, R. H., *In Search of Excellence* (Harper and Row, 1982)

Russell, P., *The Brain Book* (Routledge and Kegan Paul, 1979)

Smith, M. J., *When I Say No I Feel Guilty* (Bantam, 1975)

Townsend, R., *Up the Organisation* (Coronet, 1978)

Webb, C., *Communication Skills – Talk Yourself into a Job* (Papermac, 1979)

Video Arts, *So You Think You Can Manage?* (Methuen, 1984)

——, *So You Think You're in Business?* (Methuen, 1986)

Index

Index